WHAT IS YOUR I.Q.
(Ice Quotient)?

Test it with these questions:

• Which two NHL players went to law school and played big-league hockey at the same time?

• How did a spinning wheel bring Gilbert Perreault to Buffalo instead of Vancouver?

• What does sports' mod-man, Ken Harrelson, think of his hockey counterpart, Derek Sanderson?

• Who is the second-best defenseman in the NHL?

• Where will the NHL expand next?

You may not be in the "hockey genius" category yet, but you will be after finding the answers to these and other questions in

HOCKEY STARS OF 1972

STAN FISCHLER, author of a syndicated column, "Inside Hockey," also appears weekly in *The Sporting News* where he writes "Speaking Out On Hockey." He has written numerous books including *Bobby Orr and the Big, Bad Bruins, Strange But True Hockey Stories,* and *The Flying Frenchmen*. He lives with his hockey-writing wife, Shirley; pet puli, Chazy; and pet cat, Sybil, in New York City. He is still trying to perfect the art of watching hockey without suffering from hypertension and chronic puckitis.

HOCKEY STARS OF 1972

STAN FISCHLER

Research Assistant
FRANK BROWN

PYRAMID BOOKS • NEW YORK

To Toots, Whose Excellence Frightened The Bad Guys

HOCKEY STARS OF 1972

A PYRAMID BOOK

First printing, October 1971
Second printing, November 1971
Third printing, January 1972
Fourth printing, March 1972

Pyramid Books are published by Pyramid Communications, Inc. Its trademarks, consisting of the word "Pyramid" and the portrayal of a pyramid, are registered in the United States Patent Office.

Pyramid Communications, Inc., 919 Third Avenue, New York, N.Y. 10022

TABLE OF CONTENTS

JUDGING by all pre-season polls, 1970-71 was to be the year of the Boston Bruins.

The Stanley Cup champions of May 1970 were believed to possess the armament for a dynasty. Some Boston dreamers suggested it would last for a decade, at the very least. They were correct—for 11 months.

East and West Division foes were terrorized by the Boston attack which machine-gunned 399 goals over a 78-game schedule. The Bruins finished atop the East by a fat 20 points and, for all intents and purposes, eliminated the New York Rangers two months before the season ended.

Abject boredom was a greater threat to the Bruins than any of their foes during the regular season. Thus, when the Buffalo Sabres upset the Bruins at Boston Garden one night late in the season it really was not *that* great a surprise.

"Our biggest problems are expansion teams like Buffalo and Vancouver," said Boston's candid center Derek Sanderson. "We can get 'up' for teams like Chicago and New York, but playing an expansion team is like a first-rate night club entertainer playing at a neighborhood bar."

The Bruins' cockiness was understandable. In Bobby Orr, they boasted the best *offensive*-defenseman in the National Hockey League. Center Phil Esposito blossomed into a profligate scorer and, man for man, "The Big, Bad Bruins" were the collective heavyweight champions on ice.

In addition there was "Terrible" Ted Green, the Bruins' boisterous defenseman, who returned to the lineup following his infamous stick-swinging brawl in September 1969 with Wayne Maki of St. Louis. Wearing a bizarre helmet to protect his once-fractured skull, Green made a courageous comeback although his speech remained vaguely impaired and the quality of his play deteriorated.

But Boston's power was so awesome that Green's errors were usually obscured by the avalanche of goals by Esposito (76), Johnny Bucyk (51), Ken Hodge (43), Bobby Orr (37) and Johnny McKenzie (31).

If the Bruins had any detectable flaws they were discovered by only the persistent few—at goal and behind the bench.

Goaltenders Gerry Cheevers and Ed Johnston, average at best, combined for a 2.65 goals against average, lagging behind Gilles Villemure and Ed Giacomin of New York (2.26) and Tony Esposito and Gerry Desjardins of Chicago (2.35).

Rookie coach Tom Johnson, who succeeded Cup-winning Harry Sinden, permitted discipline to break down toward the end of the season, with the result that his players were out of shape and ill-prepared for the playoffs. This resulted in Boston's disgrace in the opening round.

In New York it was believed the Rangers would provide Boston with an effective challenge. "We never had a better-balanced team," said manager-coach Emile Francis. "This club is capable of going as far as it wants."

The Rangers have a reputation for failing in the clutch. They have not won The Stanley Cup since 1940 and have not finished first since 1942. More embarrassing, the New York sextet has not even gone as far as the Cup finals since 1950. This reputation for non-accomplishment was brilliantly maintained by Francis, whose club settled behind Boston and was subsequently dispatched from the playoffs by Chicago.

The Black Hawks, transferred to the West Division in 1970-71 when Vancouver and Buffalo were admitted to the East, conquered their division easily. Chicago collected 107 points, 20 more than runner-up St. Louis. Then, as if to prove that the rest of the West sector was comprised of nothing more than minor-league clubs in major-league disguise, the Black Hawks shellacked Philadelphia in four straight playoff games.

Champions of the East Division the previous year, Chicago developed an ideal balance between defense and attack. The brothers Bobby and Dennis Hull scored 44 and 40 goals respectively, while the defense led by Pat Stapleton and Bill White held the enemy in check. Typical of the Black Hawks was center Pit Martin who combined offense with vigilant defensive play.

"I can't emphasize how important Martin is to this club," said coach Billy Reay. "I have great confidence in him individually and in any line on which he plays."

Martin was a vital factor in the Black Hawks' march to the Stanley Cup finals against the Montreal Canadiens and very nearly brought Chicago its first world championship since 1961. Unfortunately, a transformation took place in Montreal that was more contrasting than Dr. Jekyll and Mr. Hyde.

The Canadiens, who missed the playoffs in April 1970 for the first time in 22 years, appeared to be sinking once more. Dissension surrounded coach Claude Ruel at the opening of training camp. Veterans Ralph Backstrom and John Ferguson retired.

On November 14th Ferguson returned, but Ruel resigned on December 3rd and was succeeded by Al MacNeil, a mediocre NHL defenseman who became an assistant coach of the Canadiens.

Thanks to the ineptitude of Toronto and Detroit, the Canadiens remained in playoff contention. It was obvious that Montreal needed new faces in order to climb higher. "I'm always open for trades," said Canadiens manager Sam Pollock on January 5, 1971, "but I'm sure as hell not looking."

The Red Wings were looking, however, and on January 13, 1971 the Canadiens dispatched Mickey Redmond, Guy Charron and Bill Collins to Detroit for superstar Frank "Big M" Mahovlich. A day later The Big M scored his first Canadiens goal and Montreal was off and flying.

On February 11th captain Jean Beliveau scored a three goals in one game including his 500th career goal. The Flying Frenchmen were doing well everywhere except at the net. In March Pollock produced his ace-in-the-hole, elevating McGill University law student, Ken Dryden, from the Voyageurs farm team to play goal. "Use Dryden," advised Floyd Curry of the Canadiens general staff, "and he'll win the Stanley Cup for you." Nobody believed Curry until the seventh game of the opening cup series with Boston.

Dryden won each of his six regular season games before taking on the vaunted Bruins. The insertion of this poetry-reading rookie against the defending Cup champions was hailed as one of hockey's most daring ploys.

Even more amazing, it worked.

"Dryden is green," said MacNeil, "but he's a good goalie."

Boston won the opener at home, 3-1, but Dryden played well. In the second game, the Bruins bombarded him and amassed a 5-1 lead. But the indomitable Canadiens' spirit would not be squelched. Montreal fought back and won the game, 7-5.

"That game," said Dryden, "told us we had a chance to win the series."

Montreal won the third game, 3-1, but the Bruins rebounded with 5-2 and 7-3 triumphs. Boston needed only one more, but the Canadiens demolished Bobby Orr and Company 8-3 in the sixth game.

The final game was all Dryden's. Boston scored first but the Canadiens rallied, took a 4-2 lead and let their goalie do the rest. He held the Bruins at bay, and recorded one of the most extraordinary upsets in the history of sports.

"Their entire team played well," said Phil Esposito, "but Dryden decided the series. He never cracked, never appeared to lose confidence or be bothered by the pressure. He beat us."

Montreal's handling of a supposedly invincible Boston juggernaut was a textbook classic. "We knew we had to give Bobby Orr a lot of attention," said MacNeil. "We also had to think about their attitudes. They skated easy over the last half of the season; they hadn't been harassed; and they hadn't been forechecked enough. We had to stay on top of them, and we did. We took control."

Henri Richard, a veteran of nine Stanley Cup-winning teams, epitomized the feeling of his teammates. "This," said Richard, "is the greatest series victory of my career."

It was so great that the Canadiens suffered a near-fatal

letdown in their semi-final series against the militantly average Minnesota North Stars. Montreal eventually won the series, four games to two, but not before coach Jack Gordon's club threatened to go all the way and John Ferguson openly criticized MacNeil on the Canadiens' bench.

The Canadiens were still unsteady in the first two games of the Cup finals as Chicago, led by Jim Pappin and Lou Angotti, won 2-1 and 5-3 at home.

Back at the Forum, the Montrealers tied the series at two apiece. But their house still was not in order. After Chicago defeated them, 2-0, for a three-two series lead, Henri Richard blasted MacNeil as "incompetent."

Prior to the sixth game threats were made against MacNeil's life and he required police protection throughout the game. Yet, with all the acrimony and dissent, Montreal's skaters came from behind in the third period to win the game, 4-3.

The final game was played in Chicago before 21,000 fans on May 18, 1971. If there was a more dramatic ending to an NHL playoff few could remember it.

Chicago leaped ahead, 2-0, and appeared to have the Canadiens lined up for the knockout punch. The lead seemed safe until the last six minutes of the second period when Jacques Lemaine hurled a long, hard—but manageable—shot at goalie Tony Esposito.

"I just don't know if I saw it," said Esposito. "Maybe I did. I can't be sure. I can't tell what happened. I thought I had it."

The puck sailed over Esposito's shoulder and into the net. A few minutes later Lemaire shovelled a pass from behind the net to Richard who was in front. His shot beat Esposito to tie the score.

At 2:30 of the third period Richard buzz-sawed his way around defenseman Keith Magnuson and swerved hard right toward Esposito. "I had the puck on my skates," said Richard who nearly lost control of it "and finally got it on my stick."

When Esposito came out to meet the onrushing Canadien, Richard lifted the puck over the goalie's falling body and Montreal moved ahead, 3-2. From that point on

Dryden turned back Jim Pappin, Bobby Hull and the rest of the Chicago shooters. The Black Hawks never scored again and Montreal won The Stanley Cup.

MacNeil was hoisted on the shoulders of the very players who earlier had criticized him. His job appeared secure.

Would MacNeil continue this year?

"I will be very disappointed if he's not my coach when we come to camp in the fall," said Richard after the Cup series. "He is a decent man, a good man, and a fine coach who will be a great coach."

Just how great—at least in the NHL—may never be known. On June 10th, less than a month after his astonishing triumph, MacNeil pulled the curtain on a bizarre season by quitting the champions to take a job as manager-coach of the new Nova Scotia Voyageurs in the American Hockey League.

"I realized that coaching the Canadiens would be a tough position to hold," said MacNeil. "I don't think there's a future in it for me."

MacNeil's replacement is Scotty Bowman who resigned as manager-coach of the St. Louis Blues.

When Bowman left St. Louis he was replaced by Sid Abel, former manager of the Detroit Red Wings. Abel claims he will be "the first coach to bring the Stanley Cup to St. Louis."

Then again, considering what Ken Dryden, Al MacNeil and the Flying Frenchmen did last May—anything is possible in the NHL.

THE SEASON PRESENT

GLORIOUS songs of triumph will be heard this season from New York, Chicago, Montreal and Toronto.

Emile Francis, the general manager-coach of the Rangers, who ranks among the more excessive dreamers, will assure one and all that his New York sextet has its best chance yet at first place in the East Division and The Stanley Cup.

He has a point, to be sure. The Rangers have a big and relatively young team anchored by defenseman Brad Park, goalie Ed Giacomin and center Walt Tkaczuk. They have depth and experience; but everyone in hockey knows that the Rangers under Francis have never won a major prize—first place or The Cup. So why should it happen this year?

The Chicago Black Hawks are called "The Dallas Cowboys of Hockey" because they *almost* but don't quite win The Stanley Cup. They are expected to romp in the West Division. Fortified by Bobby Hull, Pat Stapleton, Bill White and Tony Esposito, Chicago has depth, but nothing that suggests a world championship. More than ten years has elapsed since the Black Hawks won The Cup. They haven't done it since Billy Reay became coach, and Reay will be running the club this year—so the script won't change.

Toronto has just cause for optimism. Youngsters Darryl Sittler, Bill MacMillan and goalie Bernie Parent will provide oomph to drive capable veterans Dave Keon, Norm Ullman and goalie Jacques Plante. The addition of veteran Don Marshall via the June draft will be a pivotal plus.

The Leafs could be the surprise team of the season despite an overabundance of lighter, non-hitting types. Parent's goaltending and a seasoned young defense could

13

erase many flaws. "We're 60 per cent better than we were last year," says Vice President King Clancy.

The retirement of captain Jean Beliveau and veteran left wing John Ferguson leaves the Canadiens without leadership and sock. It will be impossible to replace Beliveau.

Guy Lafleur, 6-1, 185 pound graduate of the Memorial (Junior championship) Cup-Winning Quebec Remparts, appears to be Beliveau's heir apparent.

"Guy is a great goal-scorer," said Canadiens' manager Sam Pollock. "He's big and there aren't five players in hockey at any level who pass the puck as well as he does. I see him as a first-string forward for us, plus working the point on the power-play."

But nobody knows better than Pollock that there's a big difference between Junior hockey and the NHL. Lafleur may have trouble making the grade. If so, the Canadiens will have difficulty in holding onto the Cup.

Man for man the Boston Bruins have the strongest club in the NHL. Perhaps the explanation for Boston's defeat in the Stanley Cup playoffs last spring was uttered by forward Fred Stanfield.

"People have said," Stanfield remarked, "that the best team can be beaten by somebody else."

This year Bobby Orr, Phil Esposito, John McKenzie, Ken Hodge and Stanfield are planning to prove that last year's playoffs were a mistake.

If any improvement is needed on the Boston sextet it is a tightening of discipline. The Bruins, more than any other NHL club, exhibit a Gashouse Gang atmosphere in which a player such as Don Marcotte can change his uniform number from 29 to 21 "because 29 is too heavy to carry." Coach Johnson endorsed many of the shenanigans. "Sure we have some wacky guys," he admitted. "But that's what it takes."

Johnson's permissiveness allowed the Bruins to enter the playoffs last year out of shape both mentally and physically. If he becomes vigilant this year the Bruins should be too awesome for any team to control.

Certainly Boston will not be threatened by the likes of Detroit, St. Louis, Buffalo, Vancouver, Philadelphia, Minnesota, Pittsburgh, Los Angeles and Oakland.

The Red Wings staggered through last season. Coach Ned Harkness moved up to general manager in mid-season and Doug Barkley replaced him. Harkness made innumerable trades and believes he has the nucleus of a contender. "We now have a solid young base to build on, people like Mickey Redmond, Nick Libett and Tim Ecclestone, and a leader in Red Berenson," he said.

The St. Louis Blues will have venerable Sid Abel behind the bench this year, replacing Bowman who went to Montreal. "I don't think there'll be that much difference between me and Bowman in coaching," said Abel.

Abel's potential ace is long-haired center Garry Unger, obtained late last season from Detroit for Berenson. Rookie goalie Peter McDuffe will alternate with Ernie Wakely. If McDuffe lives up to his notices, the Blues could finish second in the West.

Punch Imlach's reputation as a superior hockey mind remained intact last season when he took the baby Buffalo Sabres and guided them to a respectable fifth-place finish. It's doubtful that his collection of mediocre skaters surrounding ace Gil Perreault can do better this year. Likewise, the Vancouver Canucks, who depended so heavily on captain Orland Kurtenbach last season. The Canucks finished sixth in the East, and can only hope to do better if draft choice Jocelyn Gouvremont bolsters their sieve-like defense. Whatever happens, Vancouver can count on sellout crowds throughout the year in what is the new hockey goldmine of the NHL.

Riddled with dissension, the Philadelphia Flyers dropped Vic Stasiuk as coach last June and replaced him with Fred Shero, an eminently successful minor league coach. The Flyers also obtained a prize in the June draft, defenseman Larry Brown of New York. The goaltending of Doug Favell and Bruce Gamble should be more than adequate, but scoring remains a problem unless young Rick MacLeish matures quickly.

The first West Division club to reach the Stanley Cup semi-finals, Minnesota's North Stars have added an efficient two-way skater in Bob Nevin, dealt to the Stars by New York for Bobby Rousseau. If Murray Oliver can deliver a regular season effort to match his playoff performance, Minnesota could challenge St. Louis for second in the West.

Too many senior citizens weigh down the Pittsburgh Penguins roster; and 42-year-old Tim Horton, drafted from the Rangers, will not change matters. The Penguins require a scoring burst from young Greg Polis and fast development from Rene Robert. Goalie Les Binkley, one of the most underrated netminders in hockey, must avoid injuries if Pittsburgh is to reach the playoffs.

The Los Angeles Kings have rotted under the ownership of Jack Kent Cooke and there is little to suggest better times this season. A surplus of jaded veterans and a paucity of quality overall should consign the Kings to subterranean depths once more.

In Oakland, owner Charles Finley has given rookie manager Gary Young three years to produce a winner. Young came off with 22-goal Wayne Carleton from Boston in the draft. Carleton won't turn the trick nor will anyone else in the Golden Seals patchwork lineup. Only *CARE* packages will help.

Unless Bruins coach Tom Johnson goofs again, both strategically and psychologically, Boston should decisively beat off challenges from New York, Montreal and Toronto, finishing atop the East once more. Remembering the embarrassment of 1971, the Bruins can be expected to buckle down and wipe out all opposition enroute to the Stanley Cup—barring, of course, serious injury to Hart Trophy-winner, Bobby Orr.

The contest for second, third and fourth places, unless all signs fail, will conclude with New York second, followed by Montreal and Toronto. However, the differences are so imperceptible that an injury here or there could cost a team one or two rungs in the standings.

Revitalized by young blood, the Red Wings will be the most improved team in the East while Buffalo and Vancouver should remain the same as last year.

Once again Chicago will ride herd on the West, pursued by Minnesota, St. Louis and Philadelphia. Take your pick for second, third and fourth. Pittsburgh, Los Angeles and California (Oakland) will no doubt battle keenly, if not too well, to stay out of the cellar. Any one of them could qualify for the Booby Prize.

The NHL has been riding a treadmill to oblivion in its attempt at creating parity. Boston, Montreal, New York, Chicago and Toronto remain the top-heavy rich while the other clubs continue to starve for talent.

Whatever the case, television is providing pro hockey with a popularity it never enjoyed before. Sellouts are guaranteed everywhere except Oakland, Los Angeles and Pittsburgh, and new cities are clamoring to join the NHL. The fact that quality is low fails to diminish the fans' enthusiasm. If nothing else, hockey 1971-72 will be a hit at the gate.

THE PERSONALITIES

RED BERENSON When Gordon "Red" Berenson, the scholarly center with the educated stick, was traded by the New York Rangers to the St. Louis Blues in November 1967, the deal was largely ignored. In those days the name Berenson commanded neither respect nor awe.

But when Berenson was dealt from St. Louis to the Detroit Red Wings early in February 1971, the news resounded with the impact of a thunderclap. In less than four years the anonymous redhead from Regina, Saskatchewan, emerged as the Babe Ruth of St. Louis hockey, the man who put the Blues on the ice map—and into the Stanley Cup finals.

It was Berenson who scored six goals in a single game against the Philadelphia Flyers; who became the first superstar of the National Hockey League's expansion West Division; and who graced the cover of *Sports Illustrated*. "The Red Baron" of the Blues, as he came to be known, was in a class with Bobby Hull, Gordie Howe and Jean Beliveau—the big-league galaxy.

Then, without warning, he was traded away by the very team which coveted him so dearly. It was the shot heard round the hockey world.

The precise reasons for the trade may never be known, but its repercussions lasted right into the 1971-72 season and may be heard for years to come. Berenson claimed the deal was simply a union-busting move on the part of the Blues' front office.

"I think the Blues traded me because I'm president of the NHL Players' Association," said Berenson. "I don't know why the Blues should be uptight about the association, but I'm convinced I was dealt because of that Needless to say, I'm shocked and disappointed."

So were the hockey fans in St. Louis. They were hardly ecstatic to learn that the Blues obtained Garry Unger and Wayne Connolly in exchange for Berenson and Tim Ecclestone, who also went to Detroit in the deal. Even the Blues' front office acknowledged the flak.

"I don't blame the fans," said Sid Salomon III, Executive Vice President of the Blues. "If I were on their side of the fence, I'd probably be writing or phoning my criticism. But we weren't trading for today, tomorrow or the next NHL season. We were dealing for the next ten years. We believe Unger is the kind of man we need to build a Stanley Cup-winner."

A few hundred miles away, in Olympia Stadium, Detroit, manager Ned Harkness of the Red Wings was saying virtually the same thing about Berenson. Gordie Howe, the patriarch of Detroit hockey, was close to retirement and Red was to be the club's new leader.

"In Berenson," said Harkness, "we not only have a man with tremendous leadership qualities, but a real smart center who also plays left wing."

Red found himself at home in Detroit in more ways than one. He had B.A. and M.A. degrees from the University of Michigan and, of course, played much of his college hockey in that area.

When Berenson made All-America at Michigan the late Jack Adams, Detroit's vitriolic manager, attempted to lure him to Detroit. But the Montreal Canadiens owned his rights at the time and had no intention of releasing their prospective ace. Curiously, the Canadiens often seemed indifferent to Berenson once he moved up to the NHL in 1961-62.

Berenson's good head wasn't always appreciated. Montreal's Toe Blake underplayed Red and Berenson insists he never got a good chance to prove himself. "I was a different kind of player compared with the ones Blake was accustomed to. He knew I was a college man—not that I consider myself an intellectual, I don't—and I don't think he believed I could make it. When your coach is thinking that way, your chances are not too good."

But Berenson hardly saw more ice when he was traded to the Rangers. At first it seemed he'd be the number one center but an injury sidelined him and his place was taken by Orland Kurtenbach; every time he made a comeback he'd suffer another injury and the word—unfairly—made the rounds that he was brittle.

Curiously, most of Berenson's excitement occurred off the ice when he was a Ranger. For example, there was the time he and a friend went out in a 26-foot motorboat for a spin off Long Island. By the time the vessel made it into the deeper part of the ocean the motor conked out. It hardly looked promising for Red and friend.

"There's fog," he recalled, "and I'm seasick, and here's my pal sitting in the stern lapping up brandy. There are no oars and no anchor. Twice out of the fog there comes an ocean-going craft that misses us by less than 30 feet."

The odyssey had a happy ending. After priming the engine several dozen times, Red finally got it to work and steered the craft safely back to shore. By now it is almost imperative that a hockey team take out boat wreckage insurance for Berenson because his affinity for boats—and boating disasters—is worrisome.

Another time he went fishing in one of his favorite camp areas, a distant sector of British Columbia. He was accompanied by Don Miller, a sales representative, and they were making their way in a small dinghy no more than 12 feet long. Here's how the saga unfolded in Berenson's own words:

"We had a 10-horsepower motor on the back, which is pretty monstrous power for such a little boat. All of a sudden, the motor exploded and tore off the back of the boat. Water poured in. This was a mountain lake fed by glaciers. Very cold. Mountains pitched down to the surface, which means there wasn't much shore."

To save themselves, the men moved to the front of the boat, keeping it partially afloat. They had one lifejacket and one paddle. Nothing else.

"I can swim," adds Berenson, "but we were 50 yards from shore and I'd heard that in water that cold you couldn't survive more than three to five minutes. So I picked up the oar and began paddling—furious as hell! But we started drifting toward a 70-foot waterfall. I wasn't scared at the time, that came later. All I was thinking about was paddle, paddle. At last we managed to angle away from the falls. We got to shore and, as things turned out, the only thing I got was wet feet, and sweat from paddling."

Before they could retrieve the motor it sank. The next day a diver was summoned as part of a salvage operation. When Berenson remembers what happened next a shiver or two curls up his back. "Before the diver was to go down, they put a rock on a rope to measure how deep the lake was. The rock went down 400 feet without touching bottom, so the salvage operation was called off."

Berenson didn't cause that much excitement during his two months in Detroit last season, but the Red Wing management is convinced the best is yet to come. As for the Blues, manager Scotty Bowman said he dealt Berenson for Unger because "you have to give value to get value." Ironically—and, perhaps, not surprisingly—Bowman quit the Blues last spring in a dispute with Salomon.

Only the seasons to come will determine who *really* obtained the most value in the memorable deal for Red Berenson, pro hockey's most celebrated unknown.

YVAN COURNOYER Montreal's Canadiens are known as "The Flying Frenchmen" and nobody wearing the "*bleu* (blue), *blanc* (white) *et rouge* (red)" uniform flies faster than Yvan Cournoyer, the compact right wing.

During the 1970-71 season, Cournoyer, who resembles Buster Brown, was the second best scorer on the Stanley Cup champions with 37 goals and 36 assists in 65 games. It was a considerable improvement over his previous year's mark of 27-36-63 and it proved that hard work often pays dividends.

"Before training camp started," said Cournoyer, "I did a lot of running to get into condition. I also changed from the curved-blade hockey stick back to the straight blade and I decided that I would have to shoot more often."

The results were never more obvious than in the Stanley Cup opening round with Boston, the heavy favorites. Cournoyer's effectiveness helped upset the Bruins in seven games.

"You can't scare Cournoyer off the puck anymore," said Boston center Derek Sanderson. "He showed me a lot of courage in that series."

Cournoyer also took boxing lessons during the Summer of 1970. "I did it," Yvan explained, "to get in shape and improve my timing."

Likely there were other reasons for Yvan to learn the manly art of self-defense.

For example, when Yvan takes his place on the forward line he is at a disadvantage. A built-in disadvantage. Cournoyer is 5-7 and weighs only 169 pounds, which leaves him at the mercy of the far larger, might-makes-right bullies of the NHL. "Many times," he admits, "I wish I were bigger because there are some guys I'd like to lick."

Guys like Glen Sather who regularly takes potshots at Cournoyer and some of the other smaller Canadiens. After one game in which Sather had taken a number of liberties with Cournoyer and the rule book, Sather put the Canadiens down, saying, "You can intimidate those guys. I talk to them all the time. I tell them they better not turn their backs on me. Things like that."

Sather went after Cournoyer in the opening game of the 1969 Boston-Montreal Eastern Division Stanley Cup playoff series, bloodying his nose before the game was two minutes old and sending him to the infirmary for the rest of the period. But if tactics like these are designed to intimidate, then Cournoyer insists they're not working. "All they do," he says of his tormenters, "is make me mad. And when they get me mad, I play harder. Sure, these guys might take care of me in a fight. I'm used to that. It really doesn't hurt my game. No, I don't care too much about it."

It would not seem wise to rile Cournoyer and make him play harder, for he is formidable enough when he's at peace with the world. His game is offense, and his arsenal includes roadrunner speed, excellent maneuverability, and, most important, a high velocity slap shot. Despite all the bullying, Yvan played in 65 regular-season and 20 playoff games, hardly possible from a man with a delicate constitution.

Cournoyer dishes out punishment with his slap shot rather than his fists. In a Stanley Cup meeting with St. Louis in 1969 he almost put the entire Blues' defense out of commission with a series of sizzling drives.

Cournoyer swept in toward goalie Glenn Hall and let fly. Down went St. Louis defenseman Al Arbour, writhing in pain as though struck by a bullet. The puck slid back to Cournoyer. His stick blurred again, and this time defenseman Barclay Plager toppled over. The puck came back to Cournoyer once more, and he chopped it past the suddenly lonely Hall before the All-Star goalie could move. It was vintage Cournoyer, good enough to make Blues' managing director Lynn Patrick strain for superlatives. "The best goal-scorer on the power play I've ever seen was Camille Henry," Patrick said. "But now I have to say Cournoyer is just as good."

Similar praise came from Detroit goalie Joe Daley, "His shot is right up there with Bobby Hull's," says Daley. "The thing about Yvan that worries me is he can put the puck all over—high, low, you name it—with terrific accuracy."

Cournoyer's future looks bright, indeed, with one obvious reservation. "If he can manage to take the abuse without cracking," says one veteran observer of the Canadiens, "then he could be a 50-goal man like Bobby Hull and the Rocket." The Rocket is, of course, Maurice Richard, who still has demigod status in Montreal. Often a critic of today's hockey and today's players, Richard admits that Yvan could hold his own in any era. "He's not too big, but he shoots on net all the time and he's very fast," Richard said.

Shooting and skating have been Cournoyer's main interest in life since he was a kid in the French-speaking town of Drummondville, Quebec. When he was 14, his family moved to Montreal and he quickly climbed hockey's sandlot ladder, winding up with Lachine, a powerful team in the Canadien-sponsored Metropolitan Junior League.

NHL scouts had heard good things about the little kid with the big part in his hair, but they really took notice after the final game of a Lachine-Verdun series. Yvan's club was trailing by one goal with less than a minute remaining when he captured the puck behind his own net. Bobbing and weaving, he skated around the opposition and shot the puck past the Verdun goalie. Then he scored the winning goal in sudden-death overtime.

Cournoyer soon graduated to the Junior Canadiens, a regal teenage version of the parent club. Claude Ruel was his coach then as he was later with the NHL Canadiens. "I could tell right away," says Ruel, "that he had the same scoring knack as the Rocket. I told him to shoot even more, to strengthen his shot."

Yvan went home to his father's machine shop, probed around for some scrap steel and designed some shot-improvers. "I made a couple of steel pucks," he recalls, "about two pounds each. Then I went down to the basement and shot them at heavy carpets lined up against the wall." The exercise may have weakened the foundations of the house, but it strengthened his wrists. By the following winter he had a much better shot.

This improvement was well timed. The Canadiens were scanning the junior-hockey horizon for future heirs to Henri Richard and Jean Beliveau, the reigning French-Canadian scoring titans. They called Yvan up for a five-game tryout in the 1963-64 season and he scored in his first game. "He pounced on the puck like a cat," said Beliveau. However, coach Toe Blake was less enthused. He gave Yvan part-time work during his rookie year, 1964-65, and Cournoyer scored only seven goals. "But I never let down," says Yvan, "because when you let down you're finished."

A season later he scored 18 goals, but still was used almost exclusively on the power play. By 1966-67 he was up to 25 goals, but Blake remained critical of Yvan's defensive play. Then the coach decided to gamble and use him as a regular right wing. Surprisingly, Cournoyer's defensive ability immediately improved. "Toe kept harping at it," says Yvan, "and I kept working at it."

But it was his goal-scoring that earned him his keep.

Cournoyer scored 28 goals in the '67-68 season, then took a giant leap up to 43 in '68-69. In fact, he scored No. 40 with eight games still to go in the regular season, prompting some talk about the possibility of his joining the elite 50-goal club. However, Yvan didn't even want to think about it. "If I decided that I had to score 50," he says, "every time I missed a goal I'd brood over it. That's no good. If you keep brooding you stop getting your chances. Each year I passed my record from the year before, so if I score 44 this year I'll be glad. As for 50, I don't like to think about it."

Ironically, one of Cournoyer's major assets—his skating speed—may have been responsible for his failure to score 50 goals. In the 1969 Stanley Cup semifinal series against Boston, for example, he missed four breakaways because he was moving too fast. "I've had problems with goals I didn't get on breakaways," he admits. "But I have a theory about breakaways—the more time you have to think about what you're going to do, the more things there are to think about—and that's when you make a mistake."

Yvan made a mistake early in the 1969-70 season, getting in front of a flying puck at The Forum. It broke his nose and sidelined him for two weeks. If there was any consolation, it was that the accident enabled him to spend some time at the office of the Norman Street Realties and Metro-Flame Oil Company in Montreal, which has a name plate on the desk reading, "Yvan Cournoyer, President." Apart from hockey, his business career is the major preoccupation in Yvan's life. "Right after practice I hurry to my office. There are many things to be done."

Montreal General Manager Sam Pollock would like Yvan to become leader of the Canadiens in the post-Beliveau years, now that the distinguished captain has finally announced his retirement. Of course, Beliveau is a hard act to follow. "If the players want a guy and look up to him, he is the leader," Cournoyer says. "I don't know if that would happen to me, or if we'd all want somebody else."

The mark of a leader is self-confidence. Yvan has a quiet, but growing faith in himself that sometimes surfaces in odd ways. Once, after a victory in which he had scored his sixth goal in the Canadiens' last six games, Cournoyer opened a soda bottle with the blade of his skate, prompting a Montreal trainer to warn, "Keep doing that, and it'll hurt your skating."

Cournoyer just stared, then said, "It hasn't yet and I'm not going to start doing anything different now."

Which was untrue. Cournoyer is doing something different now—he's hitting back when he's assaulted. In March 1969 at Madison Square Garden, Ranger defenseman Brad Park—five inches taller and 20 pounds heavier than Yvan—announced his desire to fight by skating into Cournoyer full speed.

"I'm not the kind who hits first," Yvan said, "but the guy dropped his gloves so I couldn't back up. I dropped my gloves and we started swinging."

The first blow was delivered by Cournoyer and it stunned Park. "I gave him a good shot," Yvan remembers, "I really liked it."

But Park landed the next punch and deposited Cournoyer on the ice. "My feet were too close together," he explains, "and I couldn't dig in. That's what happens when you don't know how to fight."

To most spectators it was just another hockey brawl, but *Montreal Star* sports editor Red Fisher perceived a deeper meaning to it. "Mark this down as the day a growing boy became a man," said Fisher.

Cournoyer's performance during the following seasons proved that statement. Sanderson repeated it last spring as Yvan made 10 goals and 12 assists during last year's Stanley Cup playoffs.

Only Frank Mahovlich and Bobby Hull did better, and they are mighty big men.

KEN DRYDEN In the late 1920s, a tall man with a furrowed brow emerged as something of a phenomena when he entered Harvard Law School. His name was Myles J. Lane, a hockey player for the Stanley Cup champion Boston Bruins. It was the first time in the history of the sport that a National Hockey League player was able to combine both law studies with regular work.

Eventually Lane obtained his law degree and climbed the legal ladder. He now is a justice on the New York State Supreme Court.

Few observers believed that Lane's accomplishment ever would be duplicated—until last spring. Ken Dryden, a 6-4 product of the Toronto neighborhood hockey system, combined studies at McGill University Law School in Montreal while playing goal for Les Voyageurs, the American League farm team for the NHL Canadiens, in the Fall and Winter of 1970-71.

With the season nearly over, the Canadiens promoted Dryden to the majors. He won the last six games of the season and led the Canadiens to an almost completely unexpected Stanley Cup Victory.

He was voted outstanding performer in the playoffs. Legal education was always on Ken's mind, "We congratulate you," his dean said before the start of the Chicago-Montreal Cup finals, "but to be fair, we can offer no special favors. Now, when do you propose to take your final exams?"

From September 1970 through February 1971 Dryden was able to obtain enough law school credits to postpone his exams until August when the ice melted. His foes would prefer him to remain in school forever.

Phil Esposito, in an unusual tribute, called him a giraffe of a goaltender who reminded Phil of his brother, Tony, the Black Hawks' crack goalie. "He plays a lot like Tony," said Esposito. "He flops around a lot, goes down and gets up, and does everything. The only thing, though, is I don't have him figured like I do my brother."

Boston's Derek Sanderson called Ken, "four-story goaltender." Montreal fans compare him with another big Canadiens' goaltender—Bill Durnan, the Vezina Trophy winner of the 1940's.

"He reminds me of Durnan," said teammate Henri Richard "especially the way he gets in front of shots to make impossible saves. He drops down like Durnan and then murders you with surprise moves from seemingly impossible positions."

Being in a seemingly impossible position has been the story of Dryden's life ever since his days at Cornell University when he had to decide on either pro hockey or law school. Dryden's predicament dates back to May 1969 when the hulking young man with the mild, handsome face sipped turkish coffee in Uncle Tunoose, a Middle Eastern restaurant on Manhattan's upper Broadway. He talked about how the rioting was mishandled at Cornell University; how the Vietnam war was growing more tragic every day; and about the meaning of life.

Once in a while he mentioned hockey. He still didn't know whether he belonged—spiritually or competitively—in professional sports. At the time Sam Pollock, manager of the Montreal Canadiens, very much wanted Dryden.

"It's funny," Dryden told his friends, "sometimes I feel impulses leading me to pro hockey and other times I think I should simply go to law school and forget pro hockey altogether. One thing is certain—I couldn't do both and expect to play meaningful hockey for the rest of my life."

Exactly two years from the day he uttered those words Dryden was being hailed as, perhaps, the most phenomenal personality the National Hockey League has known—a scholar at McGill Law School; A former three-time All-America from Cornell; an activist aide for consumer advocate Ralph Nader; and the man, who more than anyone, sparked the renaissance of the 1971 Stanley Cup champion Montreal Canadiens.

After all, he played just six meaningless NHL games

when coach Al MacNeil picked him to start against Boston.

Absurd? Not in the eyes of the Bruins who soon realized the 23-year-old Toronto native was both competent and well poised in the Cup pressure cooker.

"Dryden doesn't intimidate you," said Boston forward John McKenzie, "he just stays cool all the time and never gets frustrated. That hand of his is something else."

Dryden's big left hand showed the Bruins that nabbing flying pucks was, as Ranger goalie Steve Buzinski once observed, as easy as pickin' cherries off a tree. But when the Bruins routed Ken 6-3 in the fifth game the Boston critics figured the kid was finished.

"The Canadians have to go with Rogatien Vachon," said ex-NHLer Cal Gardner who does sportscasting in Boston. "He's got the experience." MacNeil refused to yank Dryden and was backed by his boss, Pollock.

"This kid is a great goaltender," said Pollock. "We knew that when he was at Cornell. We took a chance on him this year and look what he's done. How can anybody give up on him now? How can anybody ask more from him?"

Dryden turned back hockey's most awesome scoring machine both in the sixth game and in the terrifically tense finale.

"The credit goes to their whole team," said Phil Esposito, the NHL's leading scorer, "but if one man stands out it's Dryden."

Ken seems untouched by the swirl of acclaim, like a man fishing quietly on a desolate lake.

"Pressure is all relative," he remarked in that pleasantly pedantic style which sets him apart from the average monosyllabic hockey player. "Everything that is new is a challenge. I don't think there was any greater pressure here than with the Canadian National Team."

While fans gnaw on their fingernails and nervously watch him play, Dryden is able to remain calm because of his scale of values. To him hockey is important but not THAT important.

"Ken has always believed in his schooling first and then hockey," said Mrs. Margaret Dryden, his mother, an ex-schoolteacher in Toronto. "With him Cornell always had precedence over the NHL."

That's why Dryden shunned the Canadiens after graduating from Cornell in 1969 with a Bachelor of Arts degree in history. Instead, he joined the Canadian National Team. When the Nationals disbanded Pollock moved in with an attractive offer.

They signed him with their American League farm team, Les Voyageurs, and agreed he could practice only once a week with the Montreal-based club. This would allow him to continue his law studies at McGill, which he did. By Christmas 1970 he had only played five AHL games.

"After Christmas," said Ken, whose older brother Dave plays goal for Buffalo, "I had an easier schedule at school, so I agreed to play full-time for the Voyageurs, which meant road trips to Cleveland, Springfield, etc."

Soon the word moved along the hockey grapevine that the 6-4, 215 pounder was a better goaltender than he was a student, and he was one helluva student.

Ken's superiors practiced clever psychology in easing him into the majors. "For starters," he explained, "they had me playing on the road against expansion teams. This meant there wasn't the tension I might have felt if I had played at The Forum in Montreal. By that time I had a feel for NHL shooting and my only problem was learning to concentrate more intensely than I had been either in college or the American League."

Several of the hard-bitten pros on the Canadiens acknowledged the lanky kid. "You've got to give him credit," said captain Jean Beliveau. "It's not easy to break into the league at the end of the season."

John Ferguson remarked that Dryden was the best goaltender at training camp. "He's poised and mature," said Ferguson. "He doesn't get shaken by incidents on the ice that would bug other young goalies."

Ken admitted that sudden fame has its enjoyable moments such as the news that he was selected April's "Life Saver of the Month" for saving the Canadiens in the Bruins series.

"What gives me a kick about all this attention," he said,

"is the chance to meet people. I like that part of it and I hope I like it five and ten years from now the way some of my teammates do."

Finally, it was the finals. Two straight wins by Chicago and Arthur Wirtz, boss of the Hawks, was talking about how he was going to throw "the biggest victory celebration you ever saw" when his club won the Cup.

"Sometimes," said Dryden, "when I'm out there, I think 'Well, this is a situation I've thought about before. I'm facing Bobby Hull. Can I stop him?'"

He stopped Chicago in the third and fourth games, but the Black Hawks won the fifth and appeared winners in the sixth game, too. Then Montreal bounced back late in the game to triumph, 4-3. One game on Chicago Stadium ice, May 18th, would decide it all.

"Our trouble," said Dryden before the climactic match, "was that we've gone into Chicago thinking 'Well, we only have to win one in Chicago, so it would be nice to win tonight; but if we don't we'll have another chance." Which is really bad thinking.

"As for myself, I was taking shots from the Hulls and the others; I knew it was possible to stop them."

Dennis Hull did score for Chicago and so did Danny O'Shea. Dryden wondered whether his mates could come back as they did against Boston. They did. They tied the score and went ahead; then it was a question of how good Dryden could be.

How good is flawless? That's how good he was. Chicago never scored again and when it was over the Beliveaus, the Richards and the Tremblays hugged and squeezed the goliath. The young kid from Toronto was a champion like the rest of them.

"All you think about is winning," said the grinning lawyer-to-be. "And the feeling of winning is so great that everything else comes from it."

It was almost irrelevant to add that Ken Dryden was voted the Conn Smythe Trophy as the most valuable player of the 1971 Stanley Cup playoffs.

Someday he also may be acknowledged as the National Hockey League's most valuable acquisition during its vital expansion years. Even Myles J. Lane, the Supreme Court Justice, might acknowledge that.

PHIL ESPOSITO Phil Esposito, the sloe-eyed gangly Boston Bruins center, sometimes must wonder just what he has to do to obtain respect as a National Hockey League star. Last season, for example, he set a new big-league scoring record with 76 goals and 76 assists in 78 games.

Yet, at the end of the season Phil's critics hung a banner across the upper reaches of New York's Madison Square Garden. It said: *"Esposito, A Product of Inflationary NHL Expansion."*

The point was quite obvious. If not for the California Golden Seals, Los Angeles Kings and Vancouver Canucks, Esposito hardly would have been able to break the scoring records made by Maurice "Rocket" Richard and Gordie Howe.

The point was underlined during the Stanley Cup playoffs when Esposito was confronted with the Montreal Canadiens in a seven-game series. He performed like a mediocre skater.

Needless to say, Esposito refuses to believe his critics. Last spring he blasted the anti-Phil claque during an interview with *Newsweek* sports editor Pete Axthelm.

"They talk about how the game has slipped," Esposito complained to Axthelm; "they talk about Richard's 50 goals in only 50 games; but they don't mention that it happened in a war year—when the talent was as diluted as it's ever been.

Nobody can question Phil as the best center in hockey. His credentials include election to the NHL's First All-Star Team and the Art Ross Trophy. He's also the league's leading scorer.

"They say I needed more games to set my records. But

I got 48 goals in our first 50 games, and 64 in our first 70. Maybe I never would have scored 60 goals in the old six-team league—but who knows? All I know is you don't hear guys like Bobby Hull mouthing off about expansion."

Players like Hull don't mouth off about expansion because it is in their best interests to keep quiet. The fact is that Rocket Richard's foes were considerably better than the minor league types playing for today's NHL expansion teams.

Still, Esposito has favorable points to make. "The game today," said Phil, "is twice as fast as it was in the old days. The players shoot twice as often and twice as hard."

"Phil," said Bruins' chief scout Red Sullivan, "is one of the great all-time players in front of the net. He has the moves. He always comes up with the puck."

Playing on a line with rugged Wayne Cashman and equally bullish Ken Hodge, Esposito relies on his wings to outrough opponents in the corners and fetch him the puck for the *coup de grace*.

"We didn't set records because of weak opponents," said Phil. 'We did it because of our overall offensive philosophy. We hit, we get position in front of the net, we shoot, we help each other ... You know what I really think about all the comparison between our records and the older ones? I think there's never been a hockey club that could tie our skates."

That particular point was thrown in Esposito's face last spring by the triumphant Canadiens. After his team had been wiped out in the seventh and final game at Boston Garden, Esposito accepted part of the blame. A reporter had asked him if he had been frustrated.

"I don't know," he replied. "Disappointed, maybe ... let down, maybe ... kind of angry at myself ... my team ... the Canadiens deserved to win ... we didn't."

Actually, there was a time when few people believed Phil capable of the such scoring heights. He played for the Chicago Black Hawks from 1963 through 1967 with scant recognition.

Espo admits he didn't think it was very funny when he was traded by the flying Hawks to the Bruins three years ago. Boston had been last the previous year but he knew he was with a good hockey team and told coach Sinden so.

"What I missed first was Bobby Hull and Chico Maki," said Espo. "We were pretty close. One night in a game in Boston I had to hook Bobby to stop him from getting a goal. He winds up in the net. I wind up against the boards. At the time we were in front 7-2. To make matters worse, I get a penalty—only my second of the season. Bobby said, 'You big dumb oaf, are you trying to get us both killed?' What I should have done was tackle him, I guess."

Mostly, though, it's the other guys who are trying to tackle Espo. Their efforts have been inept to say the least and that explains why the Sault Ste. Marie, Ont. native with the wry grin is known as the "Espo Express."

Judging by his activities in 1970-71, Phil should continue to mow down his opponents. The "Espo Express" will score a lot this season and in years to come—whether his critics like it or not.

DOUG FAVELL One season in the early 1950's the New York Rangers were suffering through a seemingly endless slump. With the encouragement of press agent Herb Goren, Ranger manager Frank Boucher hired a psychologist-hypnotist to work over the club's burdened psyche.

The therapist massaged the minds of the New Yorkers one night, and then the Rangers went out on the ice and proceeded to blow a lead to the Boston Bruins in the final minute of play. When asked why his treatment failed, the hypnotist said: "The goalie isn't cool enough. He's gotta learn to relax."

Dr. Tracy was never invited back by the Rangers, but his theory held up. Even the game's best goalies cracked under the strain. Terry Sawchuk once walked out on the Bruins; Bill Durnan quit the Canadiens and Roger Crozier did the same thing to the Detroit Red Wings.

However, it's doubtful that puck punchiness will ever afflict Doug Favell, the peripatetic goaltender of the Philadelphia Flyers. The impish Favell also happens to be quite competent; which explains why Flyers' manager Keith Allen traded goalie Bernie Parent to Toronto last winter.

Typically, Favell interpreted the trade in a light-hearted way. "You see," Doug explained, "Bernie is two days older than I am and this team is on a youth kick. So, old Bernie had to go."

At the time, Parent was thought to be as much a fixture in The City Of Brotherly Love as Independence Hall. Nearly everyone thought Favell would be the man to go.

Defying the odds has been Doug's avocation ever since he broke into hockey in St. Catherines, Ontario, where his father, Doug, Sr., was a champion lacrosse player. His most arresting defeat of the oddsmakers was winning a spot on the Flyers in 1967. He simply had no business making the team.

The reason for this simply was that the then Philly manager Bud Poile obtained Parent from Boston in the 1967 NHL draft. Parent, after a season of big league experience with the Bruins, was considered one of the more accomplished young goaltenders in captivity. Favell, at best, was destined to play minor league hockey in Quebec City. But he had other ideas.

"I knew Bernie had so much of a build-up and he was supposed to be number one before we started," Favell said, his smile turning to a frown. "Once training camp started I knew nobody would believe in me; so I had to go out and work hard and prove myself before they shipped me down."

He out-goaled Parent and coach Keith Allen was confronted with two young goalies eager to get all the ice they could wangle. Allen favored the more experienced Parent while playing Favell only occasionally.

Most rookies relishing the idea of getting a big league salary, would wait their turn and keep their mouths shut.

Favell wasn't like most rookies. He marched into manager Poile's office and told him he wanted to play or he'd take the next plane home to St. Catherines; it was as basic as that.

"I was playing so well when I was playing, I couldn't understand why they took me out," he explained. "I was goin' crazy on the bench. I mean Bernie played well, sure, but I was playing well, too."

The Favell-Parent combine managed to lead a weak-scoring Flyers sextet to the first West Division championship in the Spring of 1968. But the Flyers decided—for reasons best known to the front office—to let Parent play most of the games in 1968-69 and the Flyers slipped to third place.

A dressing room accident in which Favell suffered a badly cut achilles tendon limited Doug to only 15 games in 1969-70 and, this time, Parent couldn't even carry the Flyers into the playoffs.

Last year Doug played 44 Flyers' games and Parent 30 until Bernie was traded to Toronto. Favell outgoaled Parent 2.66 to 2.76 and it was no coincidence that, once Parent departed, the Flyers again made the playoffs.

"Before Bernie was traded," Favell recalled, "I heard trade talk for three years. But I thought that if they traded a goalie, I would be the one. I imagine Bernie thought that, too."

It's possible that the Flyers' were more impressed with Favell's "cool" as opposed to Parent's more anxious attitude. "I can tell just by watching Bernie in a warm-up if he's going to have a good game," said Favell. "Bernie gets uptight. He's a serious type. The deal put me on the spot. I don't mind. I play better under pressure and, if things go well, I might run for mayor."

But things didn't go precisely the way Favell hoped. Late last season he suffered a mile case of amnesia as a result of an accident on ice and was barely back in form by the time the playoffs were over.

Defining Favell's form is a job in itself. Hal Sigurdson of the Vancouver Sun put it this way: "Favell flops around the goal crease like a bowlful of jelly—without a bowl!"

Manager Keith Allen put it another way: "Doug has alarming nonchalance."

Ask Favell and he'll tell you that he has no style. "All I do," he said, "is stop the puck. But if you want to get technical about it I guess I patterned myself after Glenn Hall and Roger Crozier. They both used the inverted 'V' formation with the legs spreading out to block the corners while using the glove for high shots."

Whatever the style may be, the Flyers apparently endorse it and, according to Doug, the feeling is mutual. "Some people knock this position," he said, "but I like playing goal."

ED GIACOMIN One of the more fashionable pastimes for hockey journalists was predicting when New York Rangers' goalie Ed Giacomin would crack under the strain of playing nearly every game of the long NHL season—without a face mask.

During the 1967 playoffs Giacomin folded before the big Montreal Canadiens' guns in four straight games. A year later he blew a long shot from the stick of a fourth-rate Chicago forward and the Rangers capitulated to the Black Hawks after leading the Cup series two games to none. The Italian-Canadian from Sudbury, Ontario was hardly more effective in 1969 and 1970 when the Rangers were dispatched from the first Cup round by Montreal and Boston.

No change was expected during the 1970-71 season until New York's general manager-coach Emile Francis came up with a new plan. Instead of having Giacomin play 70 games, as he did in each of the two previous years, Francis limited Eddie to 45 contests and permitted his other goaltender, Gilles Villemure, to play the remainder. In addition Giacomin wore a mask.

The plan was successful. Giacomin's goals against average was a personal low of 2.15 while Villemure's was a commendable 2.29. Their total—2.26—enabled the Ranger pair to capture the Vezina Trophy, awarded to the team with the best goaltending record. Besides, Giacomin was named to the First All-Star Team beating out Jacques Plante of Toronto, 157-111.

Some Giacomin-watchers still wondered whether he would execute his annual fold act in the playoffs. It certainly appeared that he would in the opening game of the first round against Toronto. But, gradually, Ed pulled himself together and, lo and behold, the Rangers actually made it past the first playoff round for the first time in 21 years.

Confronted by Chicago in the Cup semi-finals, Giacomin this time displayed rare courage. In the opening game at Chicago Stadium on April 18, 1970, Black Hawk ace Bobby Hull accidentally slashed the back of Giacomin's left hand. It was a nasty cut, deep and long enough to compel Francis to insert Villemure as a replacement.

"I couldn't believe how bad the injury was when he came to the bench," said teammate Brad Park. "The wound was about a quarter-inch wide and the first bandage simply turned into a bulge of blood."

But Giacomin insisted on returning. "I had no intentions of coming out," the goalie explained. "Things were going too good with the team and when they're going that way you like to stay in the game."

He did and the Rangers defeated Chicago, 2-1, in sudden-death overtime. Giacomin continued to play gallantly throughout the series in which the Black Hawks finally triumphed late in the seventh and final game. For Eddie, though, it was a personal victory because he proved that the playoff jinx no longer afflicted him. He was a new man in more ways than one.

Unlike previous seasons, Giacomin finally decided to wear a face-mask. "I always wore a mask in training camp," Giacomin explained, "and in practice. But I never found a mask that would protect my eyes without loss of vision, particularly when I had to look for the puck around my feet."

A Norwood, Mass., manufacturer eventually presented Giacomin will a suitable face-protector at the start of the 1970-71 season and, while it had some drawbacks—the perspiration dripped into Eddie's eyes—Giacomin wore it throughout the Vezina-winning campaign.

"The only objection I got was from my wife," said Giacomin. "She said that it's too hard to tell who's playing in goal when all the goalies wear masks."

If the mask hindered Eddie's vision when he perspired it certainly didn't limit his wandering from the goal crease. More than any other NHL goaltender, Giacomin has mastered the art of fielding a puck and passing it along to a teammate, thereby launching a play.

"Having him do that," said Park, "is like having a third defenseman on the ice. It's amazing how he manipulates the puck with the big goalie's stick."

To some observers it's simply amazing that Giacomin is *in* the NHL. He languished in the American Hockey League for five years before Francis visited Providence, Rhode Island in the Spring of 1965 to obtain Giacomin. Francis wasn't the only one; Giacomin was also being sought by an emissary from the Detroit Red Wings. The pair met head-on in a Providence hotel.

"What the hell are you doing here?" blurted the Detroit man.

Francis, then the rookie Ranger manager, stared him up and down disparagingly and replied: "You know why I'm here; for the same reason you are; to get Eddie Giacomin."

The Wings, Rangers and Maple Leafs had their eyes on the young goalie who was owned by Lou Pieri, president of the Providence Reds. When the Red Wing scout asked Francis how he was making out, the Ranger boss said he had an appointment with Pieri the following week.

"I made sure I was up at six the next morning," said Francis, "and got to Pieri's office bright and early. I brought along plenty of 8 by 10 glossy photos of the Rangers because I knew I wasn't getting Giacomin easy."

After the gentleman shook hands and sat down Francis extracted several photos from his dossier. The first was one of Jim Mikol, a checking forward of limited potential.

"Giacomin was a good-looking guy who appealed to the young people in Providence," said Francis. "I knew I had to offer one very handsome guy; at least for starters."

Then, he peeled off photos of goalie Marcel Paille (Providence has a large French-speaking population), a defenseman Aldo Guidolin and Sandy McGregor. Pieri gathered them up, and told Francis he had himself a deal.

Francis knew he now had himself a goalie, but what he didn't realize at the time was that it was the most important deal of his life. A few months later Jacques Plante, then the Rangers' number one goalie, quit on him and everything hinged on Giacomin's coming through.

For a time it appeared that Giacomin would blow it. He had never played a single game in the NHL and he was understandably unsure about the Bobby Hulls and Gordie Howes. His first two seasons were traumatic. He was rapped by newsmen and pelted with garbage in his own home rink. One night Francis reassured him "Next time they throw garbage, pick it up and throw it right back."

Giacomin hung tough and soon began displaying the brand of goaltending Francis had expected of him when he visited Providence. He made the All-Star Team in each of his last five NHL seasons and, each time, the New Yorkers gained a playoff berth.

"Getting Eddie from Providence," said Francis, "was the best move I've made."

No doubt Giacomin's teammates and fans will second the motion.

GORDIE HOWE It is a measure of Gordie Howe's impact on the National Hockey League that the big news on May 28th, 1971, when the All-Star Team was announced, was that for the first time in 16 years the

Detroit right wing was *not* a member of either the First or Second teams.

An All-Star Team without Gordie Howe is like the American flag without the star-and-stripes, or the Canadian flag without the maple leaf.

Howe has received—and utterly deserved—every one of the voluminous tributes delivered his way ever since he stepped into the NHL in 1946. By the end of the 1970-71 season he played in 1,687 regular season games; scored 786 goals, 1,023 assists, 1,809 points and received 1,643 minutes in penalties—each one a league record.

Having completed 25 big-league seasons, Howe collected the Hart Trophy as the most valuable player six times, the Art Ross Trophy as leading scorer six times. His durability and the fact that he has successfully spanned three distinct hockey eras has marked him unique in sports.

"He is not merely the greatest hockey player I've ever seen," says former teammate Bill Gadsby, "but also the greatest athlete."

This is not a minority view. A sports analyst put it another way: "In hockey, Gordie Howe has been incomparable. To put him in proper perspective, it is necessary to look at another sport for comparable achievements. He is the Babe Ruth of hockey."

Toronto—in an unprecedented move for an "enemy" metropolis—honored him with a "Gordie Howe Day". Toronto Mayor William Dennison issued an official proclamation which said it all for Howe last Spring:

"In these days of shifting loyalties and shallow beliefs, Gordie Howe stands out as a man who has remained loyal to his profession; although he plays for an American club, he has remained a Canadian. He is truly a man that the young people of today should aspire to emulate."

If anyone is going to emulate Howe, both as a person and a player, the chances are good that Mark, 16, or Marty, 17, his sons, will be the youngsters to do so in the near future. Marty, a defenseman, and Mark, a left wing, have played the past few years with the Detroit Junior A Red Wings. Both are regarded as potential big-leaguers and have been sought by scouts from various NHL teams.

Marty, who is built along the generous lines of Montreal defenseman Jacques Laperriere, is taller than his father and has the long reach necessary for a poke-checking defenseman. By contrast, Mark is a chunky skater who was voted the most valuable player in the Southern Ontario Hockey Association Junior A League. He also was named top forward and All-Star left wing.

The Howe Brothers played on a line with their father in a charity game last season before 11,650 fans at Olympia Stadium in Detroit. Gordie scored two goals while playing for the Junior Red Wings against his teammates on the NHL Red Wings. Mark scored once in a game that ended in a 6-6 tie with a remarkable Howe comic touch.

With the score 6-5 against the Junior Red Wings, 10-year-old Murray Howe, the youngest of the stickhandling brothers, entered the game for the Juniors, along with Vern Howe, Gordie's brother who works as maintenance supervisor at Olympia. It was little Murray who fired the puck past goalie Jim Rutherford for the tying goal.

"This was the greatest birthday present anyone could ever have," said Colleen Howe, Gordie's wife, who was 38 years old on the day of the game.

There were those who believed that Gordie possessed both the ability and stamina to remain in the NHL until his sons were capable of skating with him on the same team. But an arthritic wrist plagued him throughout the 1970-71 season.

Rumors sprouted that Gordie would turn to coaching, but he squashed them as quickly as he would flip a puck into the net. "There's no security in coaching," Howe said, "just headaches. One night when I was a lot younger I saw Jack Adams keel over while he was running our team. I remember Jimmy Skinner getting headaches when he was our coach and I know Sid Abel's ulcer acted up for some time. No thanks, coaching is not for me."

His coach, Doug Barkley, immediately endorsed Howe, even though Gordie was manacled with the wrist ailment. Barkley asserted that Gordie playing at 50 per cent of capacity was better than most of his competitors. "He also holds the record for most practices," said Barkley late last season. "He's unbelievable; there's nothing about the game he doesn't know."

If the tributes to Gordie Howe were laid end to end they no doubt could begin in his hometown of Saskatoon, Saskatchewan, wind around the globe, and end up back in Saskatoon.

For 25 years Gordie Howe was the definitive hockey player. Even his father, perhaps Gordie's most severe critic, would have had to admit that. On December 4th, 1968, after Gordie had scored his 700th NHL goal, father remarked, "My Heavens, what took him so long?"

BOBBY HULL There was a time when the National Hockey League practically belonged to Bobby Hull. He scored goals with the same ease that other players lace on their skates and he charmed the fans like an accomplished hypnotist.

Bobby Hull is no longer the king of hockey. He has been deposed by the younger, glamourous Bobby Orr. Nevertheless, Hull remains a dignitary among ice royalty.

He finished fifth in scoring last season—the only non-Bruin among the top five—and owned a very respectable record of 44 goals and 52 assists. More important, he believes there still is a lot of hockey left in his robust physique.

Thanks in large part to Hull, the Chicago Black Hawks finished first in the West Division, 20 points ahead of the runner-up St. Louis Blues. And, after Orr and his Bruins had been wiped out of playoff competition, Hull was leading the Chicago skaters in the Stanley Cup finals.

Hull scored an impressive 11 goals and 14 assists for 25 points in the playoffs, second only to Frank Mahovlich of the Montreal Canadiens. To some Hull-watchers, Bobby's goals at times were pure classics. Two of them, rescued

Chicago from elimination in the semi-finals against New York.

The series was tied two games apiece, and the fifth game was in sudden-death overtime. A victory for New York would have given the Rangers a 3-2 series edge plus the next game on home ice.

But Hull took a perfect pass from teammate Pit Martin and whipped a shot past Ed Giacomin for the victory.

After New York won the sixth game, the series moved to a climax at Chicago Stadium. This time the teams were tied in the third period when Hull was fed another perfect pass by utility forward Lou Angotti. Bobby released it the instant it reached his stick and, once again, Giacomin was helpless against the blur. Chicago was ahead to stay.

Hull played valiantly in the finals, but Montreal invented a "secret weapon" to defuse Chicago's big gun. It was rookie right wing Rejean Houle who guarded Bobby with enough diligence to keep him off balance.

Houle came to appreciate Hull's boundless qualities of sportsmanship. "If Bobby were a dirty player," said Houle, "he could throw me down on the ice and say 'that's it, kid' because he's one strong man. But he doesn't foul you. He tries to beat you with his great talent."

Guarding Hull has been a problem for years. Houle came as close to the solution as anyone.

"I tried not to get too close to him," Houle explained. "If I do, he can shove me off with his big, strong arms. I use my skating to stay out of reach and deflect the puck away from him or force him to pass. I never worked harder against a stronger man."

Houle was not Bobby's first shadow. Bob Nevin of Minnesota, Ed Westfall of the Bruins and Gordie Howe of Detroit have been the most ubiquitous. But Bryan Watson, over the years, emerged as the most persistent. An incident that took place when Watson played for Detroit portrays the kind of antagonism generated toward Hull by many of his shadows.

The Black Hawks had just scored against Detroit and it appeared that the puck either was put in by Hull or that it went in off a Red Wings' skate. "That's not your goal,"

Watson needled Hull. "The puck hit me. It's (Phil) Esposito's goal. Be a big man, give it to Esposito."

Watson's persistent chatter was getting to Hull but it wasn't 'til later in the game that he really hit a nerve. Watson raced up from behind and laid the lumber on the Golden Jet. Hull went down but not for long. He got to his feet in a few seconds and, suddenly, swung his stick over Watson's head. "My stick came around," said Hull, "and I clunked him."

It was an act of war not in the Hull tradition and he paid for it. Sid Abel, then general manager and coach of the Red Wings, laced into Hull unmercifully, as did several other Detroit players. After the game Hull walked to the medical room where a doctor was lacing 18 stitches into Watson's wound. "I meant to hit you," said Hull, "but I didn't mean to maim you."

Watson looked up, hardly mollified, and shot back: "It's a long season."

Houle's behavior was more decorous than Watson's, but no less enjoyable to Hull. "It's frustrating," he admitted, "and not my idea of how to play hockey."

Of course even Bobby will admit that his idea of how to play hockey has changed in recent years. The turnabout came after the 1968-69 season in which Hull scored a record 58 goals while Chicago finished in last place. A bitter clash with management inspired Bobby to miss the first 14 games of the 1969-70 season.

The Black Hawk brass made it clear when Hull returned in the Autumn of 1969 that he would do things their way or he wouldn't do them at all. It was a demeaning command but it was one that Hull chose to obey and, as a result, everyone connected with Chicago hockey was the better for it: Hull, the Hawks and management.

Bobby was ordered by the high command to be as zealous with his backchecking and defensive play as he was with his scoring. He was informed that he no longer would be excused from practices for personal appearances and non-hockey business. He was told very succinctly that he was just another member of the Chicago sextet and there would be no exception to that rule.

Hull accepted the new status quo and his adaptation to

the role of Mister Defense developed into one of the most arresting tales of the 1969-70 season. With Bobby back in the lineup the Hawks climbed into contention and stunned the hockey world by beating out the favored Bruins to finish in first place in the NHL's East Division.

"Bobby Hull no longer is the Golden Jet, the whirling fusilier who averaged 52 goals per season over the last four years," observed Jerry Green in *The Detroit News*. "He is better, and more valuable as a hockey player."

Bobby's adaptation carried over to the 1970-71 season and carried the Black Hawks to within one inch of winning the Stanley Cup. Chicago was leading in the final game against Montreal, 2-0, when Bobby's shot flew past Canadiens' goalie Ken Dryden. It should have supplied the Hawks with an insurmountable 3-0 lead; instead it hit the crossbar and bounded harmlessly away. Montreal later tied the score and won the game.

"That was a shame," said Hull, who had worked so hard and well. "I wanted this Cup win more than anything. I'm getting older. I may not have too many chances left." But observers have learned never to count out Bobby Hull.

DAVE KEON The Toronto Maple Leafs finished last in the East Division in 1969-70 and threatened to explore even deeper depths last season.

First, they were embarrassed by the inept Vancouver Canucks early in the season. Then they were thoroughly humbled by the Buffalo Sabres on their own home ice. There seemed little hope for a team liberally salted with rookies who were making mistakes every time they took the ice. Only one thing could rescue them—the leadership of an able and patient veteran.

Fortunately for the Maple Leafs, such leadership was

provided by Toronto's captain and sprightly center, Dave Keon. He not only scored 38 goals and 38 assists, but managed to be sentenced to only two penalties in 76 games, the fewest of any regular NHL ace.

His tireless skating enabled the underdog Leafs to take the New York Rangers to six games before being eliminated in sudden-death overtime.

Keon, all 5-9, 163 pounds of him, has been more or less in charge of the Toronto Maple Leafs for the past few years and, more or less, has been doing a creditable job.

Keon, perfectionist that he is, may not agree with that. He'll point out that a few seasons ago he came up with only 11 goals and 37 assists. "Regardless of all the contributions you make to a team," he pointed out, "you still like to score. Obviously I was disappointed with eleven goals."

There were those who suggested that time and a new collection of brawnier hockey players finally caught up with the Lilliputian Leaf center. It was hinted that maybe they were pushing Keon into more and more corners and battering his somewhat frail physique more than it could rightfully absorb. It was enough to make one wonder whether Dave Keon was through as a very good hockey player.

Keon replied three seasons ago with 27 goals and 34 assists, second highest on the Maple Leafs, and a commendable figure from any point of view. He also led the Leafs in their brief playoff adventure with the Boston Bruins.

In his first year under manager Jim Gregory and coach John McLellan, Keon became a new man in at least one way. Dave let his hair grow to hippie proportions, a factor that wouldn't have been possible under his former boss, general manager-coach George "Punch" Imlach. Under Imlach the Leaf morale deteriorated to a point of no return, and there are people who believe that Keon suffered as much as anybody.

"When guys are down," he once observed, "you've got to boost them. Keep hammering and you pound them down further. People forget that nobody starts out to play a bad season. You don't plan to look bad."

Keon has almost always looked good since he joined the club in 1960. He tasted Stanley Cup champagne four times and won the Calder Memorial Trophy as rookie of the year. He is a two-time winner of the Lady Byng Trophy for gentlemanly and effective play and also a two-time winner of the J. P. Bickell Cup as Leaf MVP. Four years ago he was voted the Conn Smythe Trophy as the most valuable player in the Stanley Cup playoffs.

"Dave's a leader," ex-Leaf trainer Bob Haggert pointed out. "He doesn't wait around for things to happen. He makes them happen."

Sometimes he finds himself in trouble, like the night he was in the middle of a major brawl between his teammates and the Rangers. Keon decided to play the mediator with somewhat dubious results.

"All I wanted to do," he explained, "was see that everything was even."

Despite Keon's well-heralded exploits over the years a considerable question remains in terms of his position in relation to the NHL's great centers.

"He is the best center in hockey," Maurice 'Rocket' Richard, the Montreal Canadiens' immortal scorer, said several years ago.

Richard will get an argument from followers of Phil Esposito but, as far as Toronto is concerned Keon is, pound-for-pound, the most gifted hockey player alive.

FRANK MAHOVLICH On January 14, 1971 *The Toronto Daily Star* ran a banner headline: "BIG M ON THE SPOT WITH HABS."

The "Big M" was none other than Frank Mahovlich, the Gulliverian left wing. He was on the spot because Detroit just traded him to Montreal, and he might be washed up.

It took four months for Mahovlich to prove otherwise. Reunited with his younger brother, Peter, an emerging Canadiens' star, Frank helped convert the Montreal machine from an also-ran in January to a Stanley Cup-winner in May.

During the grueling playoff grind, Mahovlich scored 14 goals and 13 assists. The 14 goals set a new NHL playoff record while his 27 points tied a playoff mark set in 1970 by Phil Esposito.

"The big thing," said Frank's ex-teammate George Armstrong shortly after the trade was made last winter, "is whether Big M gets off to a good start in Montreal. If he doesn't I shudder to think what could happen if the Montreal fans got on his back."

Frank, who stands 6-0, 205 pounds, was welcomed by kid brother, Peter, who soars over him at 6-4, 210 pounds. Known affectionately as "Little M," Peter quickly assured the world that Frank would help the Canadiens.

Big M put his superstar qualities to good use in the first round upset over Boston. His most memorable work was delivered against the Chicago Black Hawks in the finals. With Chicago leading three games to two, Frank rescued the Canadiens in the third period of the sixth game. Montreal trailed, 3-2, with more than five minutes gone in the period.

There was a face-off at the Chicago blue line. Captain Jean Beliveau of the Canadiens poked the puck ahead of him and Hawk defenseman Bill White attempted to capture it. The puck eluded his stick. Then Mahovlich lunged forward, took control of the puck and skated hard at goalie Tony Esposito. Frank's shot, partially blocked by Esposito, dribbled to a stop in *front* of the red goal line. It seemed that the swift skating Mahovlich had moved too fast and would never be able to reach the rubber. But The Big M jammed on his brakes hard enough to stab at the puck and push it into the net.

With the score tied, 3-3, the Canadiens were in trouble again as Rejean Houle was given a two-minute penalty. This time there was a face-off in nearly the same spot. Chicago won. Bobby Hull attempted to clear the puck, but bounced it off the boards and Mahovlich intercepted.

The Big M's radar immediately detected Little M free on the left side. He ladled a pass to Peter who cruised toward Esposito. The goalie did almost everything right—carefully moved out to cut down the angle, refused to commit himself before the shot, and stayed cool—but Peter found an opening just over Esposito's right shoulder and lifted the puck into the net. It won the sixth game.

"This was the greatest thrill of all," said Frank after sipping the victory champagne in the Canadiens' dressing room. "I played on four Cup-Winners in Toronto but being on a championship team with my brother just thrilled me to death."

Throughout the French-speaking province of Quebec, the Canadiens, normally known as "The Flying Frenchmen," were being hailed as "The Flying Mahovliches." Frank admitted that he was affected by the special spirit of playing for the Canadiens, a team that has won a record 16 Stanley Cup championships.

"The people have a special passion," said The Big M, who is of Croatian descent. "That passion makes it different."

Once, a long time, ago, Frank experienced a special passion for playing hockey when he was a young left wing with the Toronto Maple Leafs. But the passion eventually was lost because of a combination of extraordinary pressure and—at least to Mahovlich—an oppressive coach.

He suffered two nervous breakdowns when he played in Toronto. His dispute with general manager-coach Punch Imlach was so severe that neither player nor boss exchanged a word for five years. His goal-scoring dropped from a high of 48 in 1961 to an abysmal 18 in 1967. "It reached a point," said Mahovlich, lightly creasing his brow in three places, "where I felt I was beating my head against a wall. If I had to play in Toronto one more year I'd probably retire, although I like hockey and wouldn't want to leave it."

As hockey players go, in March 1968 Mahovlich was like a beat-up Rolls-Royce. Whereas his long legs once blurred him from one end of the rink to another, he now appeared indolent and weak. His booming shot was virtually muted and he was regarded as a poor risk in the NHL's used-skater market.

On March 3rd, 1968, Sid Abel, the general manager of the Detroit Red Wings, decided to take that risk and obtained Mahovlich in a complicated seven player deal that was one of the biggest in hockey.

More important than that was the fact that the trade not only saved the hockey career of Frank Mahovlich, it turned him back into a superstar. It lured him out of his social cocoon and inspired a personality transformation that would make Jekyll and Hyde seem piddling by comparison.

"I said I'd be tickled if Frank scored 35 goals in his first year at Detroit," said ex-Red Wing coach Bill Gadsby. "Thirty wouldn't have been so bad either."

But the six-foot, 205 pound Mahovlich scored 49 goals, the most he's ever scored in 12 NHL seasons. It was the most goals for a Red Wing player since Gordie Howe scored the same number in 1952-53. No Detroit player ever scored more goals in a season. It also earned him a berth on the NHL's Second All-Star Team and he was voted the number one star of the 1969 All-Star Game in Montreal.

To Mahovlich Toronto represented a haunted city. He was recognized and hounded wherever he went by fans who were never satisfied with his play. He clashed with teammates over his temporary refusal to join the Player's Association. And then there was the spectre of Imlach who bothered him more than all of the other things put together.

In Imlach's mind, Punch commanded with the authority of Napoleon, the wisdom of Socrates and the insight of Einstein. The violin-playing Leaf boss believed that all players, though constructed differently, should be treated equally. "Yeah," added one ex-Leaf, "equally bad."

When it came to Mahovlich, Imlach lost points immediately. Punch had an irritating propensity for mispronouncing his name MA-HAL-A-VICH instead of MA-HOV-LICH. Frank is a sensitive man who happens to be a connoisseur of champagne. He went to France in 1969 to bring back a few bottles of the very best *Moet et Chan-don*.

"Imlach refused to understand him," said Paul Rim-stead, sports editor of *The Canadian Magazine*. "The relationship deteriorated to the point where Mahovlich no longer could play his best hockey for the Leafs."

Mahovlich, of course, was delighted to be free of Im-lach's shackles. For years the Red Wings were renowned as a relaxed team with an obvious "joie de vivre." During playoff time manager Sid Abel would take his men to the race track rather than seclude them in some distant hide-away. Frank was aware of this but he wasn't quite sure about how the Detroit players would react to him.

"There was pressure at first," he recalled. "Some of them heard the Frank Mahovlich stories and they were wondering if they were true. And I was never the kind of guy who tried to sell myself."

Gradually, both players and newsmen began to notice the metamorphosis. The Big M began to laugh and joke with his cronies and, pretty soon, he became one of the boys. His 49 goal total in 1968-69 was the most ever scored by a Red Wing left winger. He led the team in three-star votes and scored the goal that resulted in Gor-die Howe's 1,000th assist.

With 118 goals the Howe-Mahovlich-Delvecchio line had broken the 105-goal record set in 1943-44 by the famed Punch Line of Maurice Richard, Toe Blake and Elmer Lach. Its 264 points smashed the 223-point mark set in 1956-57 by Detroit's Production Line of Howe, Lindsay and Ullman. The line, incidentally, out-goaled 118-110 Boston's crack line of Phil Esposito, Ken Hodge and Ron Murphy although Esposito finished the 1968-69 season with a record-breaking 126 points.

For Howe it was a special treat because Mahovlich was the finest left wing he had the pleasure of working with since Hall of Famer Ted Lindsay quit hockey. It also was tribute to Howe's versatility that he could mesh so easily with such different stylists as Lindsay and Mahovlich.

"I can't figure two guys being any more different," said Howe. "Ted was rambunctious. He'd lay the lumber on everybody. Frank skates for those holes. I've never seen a player who could skate for those holes better than Frank."

Mahovlich scored 38 goals and 32 assists for 70 points in the 1969-70 season. He was one of the prime catalysts pushing the Red Wings into a playoff berth for the first time in four years and appeared to be a Detroit fixture for years to come.

But the Red Wings' front office underwent a major upheaval during the summer of 1970; when Ned Harkness became coach the team descended to the lower depths of the NHL. Trade after trade was made to revive the Detroit sextet but nothing worked. Finally, Mahovlich was dispatched to Montreal on January 13, 1971.

"Maybe they thought I was part of their trouble," said Frank who had scored 108 goals in 198 league games for Detroit. "I'm as confused as anyone else. Maybe they know what they're doing. Maybe not."

Based on Frank's accomplishments in Montreal, it has to be 'maybe not.'

BOBBY ORR One of the most significant aspects of the 1970-71 hockey season was that Bobby Orr of the Boston Bruins proved his invincibility as an ice leader—by failing.

Orr's Bruins were pushed out of the Stanley Cup playoffs in the first round when Bobby suffered one of the few slumps of his career.

Supposedly, when Orr went sour the powerful Bruins had enough armament to take up the slack. But neither Phil Esposito, nor John Bucyk nor Ken Hodge was able to liberate the Bruins.

"Ever since I joined this club," said Boston goalie Ed Johnston, "Orr was our Moses."

He certainly was that during the regular season, leading the Bruins to the promised land of first place in the East

Division, 11 points ahead of the New York Rangers. Bobby, a defenseman, finished second in the scoring race with 37 goals, a record-breaking 102 assists and 139 total points.

Orr easily won the Norris Trophy for the fourth straight time as the NHL's oustanding defenseman and captured the Hart Trophy as the league's most valuable player for the second time. The only other defenseman to win the Hart Trophy was former Bruins defenseman Eddie Shore, who won the prize four times.

"In my 35 years in the NHL," said Bruins manager Milt Schmidt, "Bobby is the greatest player I have ever seen in the past, the greatest player at present, and if anyone greater should show up, I just hope the Good Lord has me around here to see him and let him be a Bruin."

Orr not only has taken on Messianic qualities for the Bruins, but for the NHL as well. In an era when big-league hockey is spreading its wings to new areas of North America, Orr remains the most saleable commodity the shinny moguls have to offer. And nobody knows it better than Orr's attorney Al Eagleson of Toronto.

"Bobby is the only player who can help out the low-drawing teams in the NHL," said Eagleson. "For example, in Oakland, Orr played there on a Sunday night and drew 10,500. St. Louis came there on a Wednesday and drew 3,000. In Los Angeles, Orr drew 12,700, the next night against St. Louis the crowd was only 7,200. Vancouver's manager says he could sell an extra 30,000-40,000 tickets when Orr is in town."

This continental adulation of Orr does not stop at the end of the hockey season. Last June Bobby visited Vancouver and, within ten hours, conducted several interviews, appeared on a talk show, spoke at a luncheon and then conducted a three-hour autograph session with kids. When asked about his position in the prime center of the NHL limelight, Orr replied:

"I never think of myself as an idol. I'm a hockey player. I enjoy the hockey. The money? I never think about becoming a millionaire, or anything. When I quit, it will be because I don't enjoy it anymore. Of course, sometimes it's a little bit tough. You sign your name and you're polite, when all you want to do is get away by yourself. But they won't let you go. I sign autographs until I go batty."

Orr receives an average of 5,000 letters each week during the hockey season. They've come in such droves that a Boston newspaper devoted two full pages to nothing but letters to Bobby Orr for most of the hockey season.

Despite his impact on the hockey world, Orr the person has often appeared aloof and occasionally surly. The fuss and fanfare has affected him a lot more than his friends and agents care to admit.

"Throughout it all," observed author Tom Dowling, "Orr remains remote and circumspect, a little abashed at all the furor unloosed in his name, like some medieval monk whose pious lifework has inadvertently overturned the status quo of which he is a contented member."

The Orr paradox was never better exemplified than last season when *Sports Illustrated* selected him as its "Sportsman of the Year." Yet, in the article author Jack Olsen depicts episodes which question the true nature of sportsmanship. At one point Olsen reports that Orr cut off another motorist while driving. Then, Bobby gunned his car the wrong way on a one-way street and, later berated a *maitre d'hotel* at a restaurant.

Whatever his off-ice behavior, Orr's deportment on the ice cannot be questioned in terms of his abilities. When he entered the NHL at age 18 he displayed the strong skating, mighty shot, unwavering courage and keen instincts that comprise the superstar. What's more, he played a vital role in changing hockey from a bush-league low-paying sport into one of the higher-salaried team games.

Until Bobby Orr came along, nobody but nobody in professional hockey—and that includes the super-dupers like Gordie Howe and Bobby Hull—earned more than $40,000. In the summer of 1968 Bobby Orr signed a three-year contract reportedly amounting to *$400,000*.

The exact figure of Orr's contract is not especially important. What matters is that this kid, even while he was still in his teens, was teaching hockey's supposedly sophisticated old pros what life was all about; and one of the first lessons is that you get paid the kind of bread you deserve. What Bobby Orr did that neither Mantle nor Lombardi nor Chamberlain did was lead the way toward the organization of a hockey player's union which has since lifted salaries to such a point, the average skater received $18,000 annually. Before Orr came along, the average was about $11,000.

Hockey's labor revolution erupted three years ago when it came time for the Bruins to sign the then 18-year-old Orr to a contract. Every 18-year-old who ever joined the National Hockey League had been delighted to sign for the salary offered by management.

The difference between Bobby and the other 18-year-olds was that he had an old friend named R. Alan Eagleson, who also happened to be a lawyer with a keen interest in hockey. Eagleson agreed to advise Orr in his negotiations and without so much as drawing a deep breath won a two-year, $75,000 contract. When veterans twice as old as Bobby got wind of the windfall they phoned Eagleson and requested his advice. It didn't take long before the National Hockey League Players Association was organized and players who once might have been jealous of Bobby, the prodigy, now were eulogizing him.

It is one thing to be a gifted athlete, which Bobby obviously is. It is another to be a wealthy athlete, which also is the case; but it's something else when you're gifted and wealthy and as perfectly wonderful as the fictitious "boy-next-door." Yet Bobby is just that and people who have been around enough to be super-cynics waste no time admitting it.

In the big-league hockey jungle, hard-bitten veterans go out of their way to "test" rookies. They'll thrust the point of their stick-blade in the stomach or they'll ram an elbow into the jaw. If the rookie doesn't hit back he's through. In a matter of months he'll be run right out of the league. When a rookie happens to be outdrawing a low-salaried veteran by two-to-one the "test" becomes even more severe.

One of Bobby's earlier tests was given by Ted Harris, a big, rawboned defenseman then with the Montreal Canadiens. Even under the most pleasant circumstances, Harris is mean and on this night he directed some of his venom at

Bobby. There were no second thoughts. The kid dropped his stick, then his gloves, and tore at Harris. The Montreal bully went down; but he was up again and, then, down a second time. Orr had "won his spurs," and Bobby hasn't backed down since.

Opponents see all things in Orr but the best of them all, Gordie Howe, believes the essence of Bobby's superiority is his leg strength.

"He's got the legs," Howe explained. "He's also got a good attitude, plenty of desire and he always hustles. He's also an awfully nice kid. In the summer of 1968 I had my two boys with me on a promotional trip to Bobby's hometown, Parry Sound, Ontario, and Bobby was dressed in a white shirt and tie. As soon as the festivities were over we went to his house and he changed into a sweatshirt.

"It was the one which had a Gordie Howe crest on the front. My boys like that."

Unconsciously Bobby's favorite word is "super." This is perfectly natural in view of his hockey-playing efforts. "Orr," says New York Post columnist Larry Merchant, "is at least hockey's sixth dimension. He is one of those rare athletes who revolutionizes his game as Babe Ruth did, as Bill Russell did. Bobby Jones once said of Jack Nicklaus, 'He plays a game with which I am not familiar.' Orr plays hockey in a way that makes old-timers feel like dinosaurs, too."

Yet, recent history has proven that with all his talents, Orr can be defused. Al MacNeil, who coached the Canadiens to the seven-game triumph over Boston last Spring, explained how the job is done.

"We chased him," said MacNeil. "We had our defense standing up at the blue line and going after him in our end. We went after him in their end. We covered points on the power plays. We didn't want him to get the puck too much and I don't think he did."

Less reverential than his fans, Orr put himself in perspective after the Boston-Montreal series. "I'm going home," Bobby said, "and practice playing hockey."

BRAD PARK Brad Park is either the second best or third best defenseman in the National Hockey League. It all depends on which voting list one consults.

In balloting for the James Norris Trophy "to the defense player who demonstrates throughout the regular season the greatest all-around ability in that position," Park finished second to Boston's super Bobby Orr in the 1970-71 race.

The New York Ranger defenseman collected 57 points, 22 more than J.C. Tremblay of the Montreal Canadiens who was third.

Yet, in the voting for the NHL All-Star Team both Park and Tremblay finished in a tie for second behind Orr, each with 121 points. Tremblay was awarded the first team berth on the strength of having more first place votes and Park, who had made the first team in 1969-70, was relegated to the second team along with Pat Stapleton of Chicago.

Park's value to the New York hockey machine is comprehensive. He specializes in puck control, stickhandling the rubber out of the Rangers' zone and devising plays that enable his forwards to obtain good scoring position. His shot is hard and accurate and his defensive skills are many.

One of Brad's specialties is the hip check, which is a rarely-used maneuver in which the defenseman thrusts out his *derriere* when an opponent approaches and hurls the enemy over his back upon contact with his hip. Occasionally, Brad will assume the "policeman" role on the Rangers' defense. Most of the time it's a serious matter but there have been comic overtones.

One night Park tried to put the slug on Pat Quinn, who could play Goliath any day without wearing elevator shoes.

This was December 21st, 1970 at Madison Square Garden. The Rangers were slugging and occasionally playing hockey with the Vancouver Canucks. And there was Park running at Quinn. Yes, Quinn, that man who once flattened Bobby Orr.

"If we were winning, 2-1," said Park, "I wouldn't have fought. And if we were losing, 2-1, I wouldn't have fought. But we were winning, 5-1 and Quinn had hit me in the chops, so I had no choice."

For a previous few seconds it appeared that Quinn would draw and quarter Park. Then, just when it looked as though Brad would topple over on his back like the penny arcade boxer, he recovered and began belaboring Quinn about the jaw and head. When the fight was over Quinn left the ice holding his head and never returned for the rest of the game.

"I think he thought I was a forward," said the 22-year-old Park, "and I think he thought a forward wouldn't retaliate."

But Park has been retaliating ever since he startled everyone—except himself—by making the Ranger varsity in 1968-69. He startled a lot more people by grabbing off that First All-Star defense berth with Bobby Orr in the Spring of 1970. And he startled absolutely no one by sharing the berth with Orr again at mid-season 1970-71.

It now has become apparent to professionals that Park not only is in Orr's class, but surpasses the Boston player in certain defensive skills.

"Park is a tremendous defenseman," said Ned Harkness, the Detroit Red Wings manager. "He moves the puck well, he rushed it, he's sound defensively. He's a great one. By comparison, Orr is more offensive-minded.

"But Brad is defensively sounder than Orr. Park turns well and is good around the net. When I saw the two of them paired together in the All-Star Game I said, boy, what a dream that is!"

It is a measure of Park's development as a professional that he is frequently being compared favorably with Orr. Vancouver Canucks coach Hal Laycoe who, oddly enough, played for both Boston and New York, suggested that Park may outlast Orr because the Bruins defenseman is more susceptible to injury.

"Park is tough and aggressive," said Laycoe. "I'd say he's likely to have a longer and more productive career than Orr."

After watching Park deflate three Canadiens at the Montreal Forum, National Hockey League President Clarence Campbell said: "That kid looks like another Fern Flaman."

Not-so-oldtimers recall Flaman as the spike-eating Toronto and Boston defenseman with a high I.Q. (injury quotient), only the injuries were not suffered by him.

Like Orr, Park learned his game in Canada's Ontario province under the Argus eye of his father who had more than a passing interest in the sport. That's where the similarity ends.

Orr was discovered and deemed a potential shinny Messiah before he was 16. Meanwhile, Park was wondering if he should have been eating more of a certain breakfast cereal. He was a wee lad who looked as though he'd be blown over by the next wind.

But he also was tough; tough enough to land a spot on the Toronto Junior Marlboros, a club that normally fed gifted stick-handlers to the NHL Toronto Maple Leafs. Which is exactly where Brad thought he'd land, if he played his shots right.

That was 1966, a year when the NHL had instituted a 17-year-old draft rule which enabled the New York Rangers to land Park and not the Maple Leafs. To say the least, Brad was stunned to the core.

"The idea of being picked up by any other team than the Leafs never occurred to me," said Park. "The Leafs were my favorite team. Ron Stewart and Bobby Nevin were with 'em then. I had heard a lot about New York as a city and the more I thought about playing there, the more I got intrigued—although my folks weren't crazy about my leaving Toronto."

His folks, Betty and Bob Park, weren't crazy about it, because they had guided and developed their son as a hockey player in Toronto a bit more intensely than most parents. Bob Park had been a kids' hockey coach for years—and still is—while Betty Park, who was a physical education instructor in the Royal Canadian Air Force during World War II, helped out on the sidelines. It was a time when neither would have dreamed that someday their son, Brad, would himself author a book, *"Play The Man"* as he has this season.

"Brad started playing hockey when he was five," Mrs. Park recalled. "He couldn't see why he couldn't play if his older brother, who was three years older, already was in the game. Brad bugged his dad until finally they let him play goal. When they found out he could skate they put him up front."

Young hockey players often hone their skills to sharpness at the cost of a destructive household. In the Park home there were constant seismic reverberations as Brad pounced pucks off shingles, steps and garage doors.

"By the time we moved to another home," said Mrs. Park, "there were more dents in the wood panelling than there were nails."

Both Bob and Betty Park kept their lines out to Brad as he moved up the hockey ladder. It was not unusual for Bob to be on the phone to Brad after an NHL game in his rookie year; always seeking to improve the boy. And Betty would get her lessons in, too.

"I'm very critical of him," she admitted. "If he doesn't hit within the first few minutes on the ice I don't think he's going to play the kind of game he's capable of playing. We always have felt that constructive criticism is helpful. Brad always needs an incentive. Needless to say, Bobby Orr has provided some of the best incentive available for Brad. A Toronto columnist remarked that had Orr arrived in another era, the praise for Park would even be more lavish.

"Bobby has had a definite influence on my play," said Park. "I began studying him in the 1968-69 season. While I was out with a broken ankle last year I saw him play twice on television and twice in person, not to mention the times I've seen him from the bench.

"One thing that impresses me is that he never panics. He slows play down and then, when he's drawn guys in, he'll bust out with his great skating speed."

Orr influenced Park in still another way—financially. Brad became involved in 1970 in the bitterest contract squabble in Ranger history when he and teammates Jean Ratelle, Walt Tkaczuk and Vic Hadfield each were separately represented by the New York firm, Pro Sports Inc.

Although Ratelle and Hadfield signed on the eve of the season's opener, Park and Tkaczuk held out until the eve of the Rangers' third game before signing. It was significant in many ways, not the least of which being that Tkaczuk and Park were close friends.

"My closest friend is Walter," said Brad. "I get along really well with him. Of course, he's real easy to get along with; he's a very happy-go-lucky guy and I am, too. And he's very funny."

Not long after Park and Tkaczuk had signed their contracts, the Rangers' dressing room was visited by Al Eagleson, counsel for the NHL Players' Association. Eagleson discussed some Association matters and then asked if there were any questions.

"Let's go to arbitration," kidded Tkaczuk.

"No, no," snapped Park, "every time I go with Walter I get in trouble!"

Brad kids about it now but the negotiating was a long, bitter and often enlightening experience for him. At one point his father, Bob, was called in as an arbitrator in the dispute.

"All through the negotiations," said Brad, "he'd bring up points that I hadn't thought of. He's got a finesse, something like Emile Francis (the Rangers g.m.-coach). He can handle people; he can explain things. He'd say to me 'well, whaddya think about that?'

"I couldn't think of an answer right off the bat. I'd go home, sleep on it and then come back with it the next day. I like to think things out before I say anything, to be sure I'm saying the right thing. My conscience bothers me when I say something I shouldn't."

His conscience shouldn't have been bothering him when it came time to demand a raise. By now it is a folk tale in New York hockey circles that Park injured his ankle February 19th, 1970, and the Rangers began their descent from first place on February 26th and very nearly wound up out of the playoffs. When Brad finally returned in late March his condition was poor but he thought he might just lift the club.

"I don't know what I'll do," he said at the time, "but I'll shake things up, you can bet on that. If I have to fight, I'll fight. And if I have to carry the puck, I'll carry the puck."

The Rangers fitted into a playoff berth on the final night of the season. One Canadian critic analyzed Park's contribution this way: "If you were to ask for a vote on the athlete whose reputation soared the highest, Park is an obvious nominee."

Unlike Orr, Park is not surrounded by aggressive huskies. The Rangers remain a razzle-dazzle pass-the-puck team that will win by finesse rather than fuss. Ever since his rookie season Park has led the Rangers in bodychecking, a fact that surprised Francis, even in Brad's sophomore year. "The kid averaged seven hits a game in his second year, the same as he did in the first," said Francis. "At first I thought it was rookie luck or his strangeness to opposing forwards that was working for him. He became our top hitter by a wide margin."

The question now is whether Park can keep the Rangers within striking distance of the powerful Bruins. Obviously, Brad believes New York can go all the way, a feeling not exactly shared around the league, particularly in New England.

But say this for the kid; he hasn't lost his perspective despite all the adulation, his face on a cereal box cover, on television and numerous promotions. He enjoys the discovery that not everybody has yet discovered Brad Park.

"It wasn't very long ago," he remembered, "when we were playing Minnesota and a writer came into our dressing room. He looked around the room and walked over toward me.

"He peered at me for a couple of seconds and finally said, 'Can you tell me where I can find Brad Park'?"

One of the more likely places in 1972 will be on the NHL All-Star Team.

GILBERT PERREAULT Perhaps the most anti-climatic event of the 1970-71 hockey season was the disclosure last May that Gilbert Perreault of the Buffalo Sabres had won the Calder Memorial Trophy as the outstanding rookie in the National Hockey League.

Almost from the moment the French-Canadian center stepped on the ice, it was apparent that the NHL was being graced with a rare and gifted young man. His strides were long and smooth, his shot was crisp and on the mark and his temperament was dry-cool.

What's more, he could produce. Oh, my, how he could produce. By the end of the season he had scored 38 goals, more than any other rookie ever had scored in the majors. His assist total was a handsome 34 for a point total of 72—also a record—placing him in a tie on the scoring list with such eminent stickhandlers as Stan Mikita of Chicago and Jean Ratelle of New York.

"There's one thing Gil still has to do," said his manager-coach Punch Imlach. "He still hasn't scored a goal against Toronto. Some day he's going to fill the net against the Leafs and I'm going to be there to enjoy it."

Imlach, who once held a similar manager-coach position in Toronto, still is smarting from his eviction as Maple Leaf boss, even though it took place in 1969. But if there has been any balm in Imlach's life it has been his acquisition of Perreault.

The six-foot, 195 pound skater was the talk of Canadian junior hockey for several years. In the 1969-70 season he scored 51 goals during the regular campaign and then added 34 in 28 playoff games. He became, in a teen-aged sort of way, what Maurice "Rocket" Richard had been to the Montreal Canadiens during the Forties and Fifties. When handsome Gil would gather the puck for the Junior

Gordon "The Red Baron" Berenson sets up play for St. Louis before late season trade to Detroit for Garry Unger.

Toronto captain Dave Keon (R) presents Gordie Howe, of Detroit, with a silver tray on Howe's forty-third birthday.

Printed in U.S.A.

St. Louis center Garry Unger (7), then with Detroit, flips shot at Boston goalie Gerry Cheevers.

Fred Barrett, Minnesota defenseman, looks at Gordie Howe. Howe eyes the puck. Goaltender Cesare Maniago has to look for his stick, which was knocked out of his hand moments earlier.

Ed Giacomin, masked in 1970-71 for the first time in his career, zeroes in on flying puck while New York Rangers teammates check Toronto's Guy Trottier.

Philadelphia goaltender Doug Favell masks his disappointment as St. Louis forward Gary Sabourin (11) shoves puck under the goalie's glove and into the net.

He flies through the air. Boston's "superman" Bobby Orr trips over Gilles Gilbert in the Minnesota crease, then lands, head under heels, on the ice.

Linesman Pat Shelter reminds Brad Park (left) of the Marquis of Queensbury Rules after New York defenseman lost his sweater in fight with Philadelphia's Bill Lesuk.

Buffalo Sabre coach and manager Punch Imlach congratulates his rookie star Gilbert Perreault (left) after Perreault had scored his thirty-fifth goal, most ever by an NHL freshman.

A Boston police officer uses his head to stop Bruins' fiery, mustached Derek Sanderson from getting to Canadien Phil Roberto (17, bottom right). Bruin teammates Don Marcotte, Gerry Cheevers, and Don Awrey (l. to r.) surround the scrappy center.

There's snow business . . . goalie Gump Worsley gets help from defenseman Tom Reid (20) in kicking out a Boston Bruin shot on the Minnesota net.

All eyes are on Canadiens' Pete Mahovlich (dark shirt) and Blues' defenseman Jim Roberts as they mix it up behind the net at the St. Louis Arena.

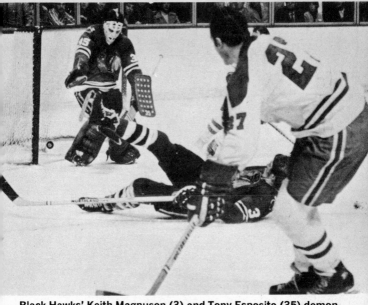

Black Hawks' Keith Magnuson (3) and Tony Esposito (35) demonstrate unsuccessful methods of goaltending as Frank Mahovlich (27) of the Canadiens watches his third period shot enter the net during third game of the 1971 Stanley Cup final series.

Hey fellas, the net's over here! Bobby Hull (9) of Chicago sends puck past Rogatien Vachon (30) of Montreal, but the disc dribbles past the goal. John Ferguson (22) and J. C. Tremblay (3) hold off Black Hawks' Eric Nesterenko.

Bruins' centerman Phil Esposito displays pucks he put into the Los Angeles net during 9-5 Boston victory. His 75 goals smashed the NHL scoring record.

Montreal's Yvan Cournoyer seems to be searching for his legs after taking a spill at Maple Leaf Gardens. Toronto's Jim Dorey looks down on the fallen "Frenchman."

Montreal goaltender Ken Dryden is up to his mask in trouble a Danny Grant (21) scored for Minnesota in last spring's Sta Cup semifinals. Defenseman Jacques Laperriere (left) and ward Frank Mahovlich (27) arrive too late.

Canadiens people in The Forum would chant, *"On veut Perreault!"* (We want Perrault!)

In pre-expansion hockey days a French-speaking player such as Perreault enjoyed an almost 90 per cent chance of landing on the Canadien's roster. But that was long ago. The normally medieval-thinking NHL owners finally realized that expansion teams need good young talent and Imlach decided to hang on to Perreault, although the temptation to deal him to Sammy Pollock, manager of the Canadiens, was immense. However, in a weak moment, Imlach allowed he would make a deal.

"All Sam's gotta do," said Imlach, "is gimme Jean Beliveau, Jacques Lemaire, Henri Richard, Jacques Laperriere, J.C. Tremblay and a few more of them."

Which explains why Gilbert Perreault checked into the Buffalo Sabres training base one afternoon in September 1970. Once he shook himself loose of the press clippings it became apparent that this was a superb hockey player.

"He looked like a million dollars on skates," said Red Burnett, the veteran hockey analyst for *The Toronto Daily Star*.

It would be easy to say that the pressure was on Perreault from the moment he skated out on the ice for Buffalo in a regular NHL game; but that's nonsense. Perreault, as so many young NHL players are realizing these days, knew that no matter what happened he was in the big-leagues to stay—at least for this season. He knew that his three-year $25,000-a-year contract meant that he was "in like Flynn" and that the talent-starved Sabres needed him more than he needed Buffalo.

So what if he didn't knock 'em dead, the NHL has become a player's market and who's going to replace Gil Perreault on the Sabres' roster? Who? Certainly not Brent Imlach, Punch's son.

Perreault came along with the usual publicity harangue. Somebody remembered that Gil's first organized team was in Victoriaville, Quebec, the very same town where a chap named Jean Beliveau learned his hockey. And then word got around that Perreault had patterned himself after Beliveau. Like Beliveau, Perreault would rather play hockey than fight, they said. Sometimes they compared him with

Bobby Orr, other times with Gordie Howe. The consensus was that Perreault was as certain to be a superstar as the rest of the members of the Buffalo roster were not.

Then, it came time to play hockey for real.

No matter how you shake it Buffalo was in a jam. Imlach's blather notwithstanding, one Toronto reviewer took due note of the Sabres' lineup and called it "the worst collection of misfits ever assembled under the guise of a big-league hockey team."

The exception, of course, was Perreault.

Less than a month after the opening whistle it had become apparent that if Buffalo had one genuinely superior hockey player it was Monsieur Perreault. Even during an abysmal Sabres' defeat—and they were abundant in the beginning—Gil emerged as a gem in a mudbath.

On October 27, for example, the Sabres were tarred and feathered, 7-2, by the Vancouver Canucks before 15,068 fans at the Pacific Coliseum. The gleeful winners were led by Mike Corrigan in the dressing room who shouted, "I guess we showed them who got the best draft picks." But, actually, it was Perreault who shone in defeat, even though he had been shackled by fellow French-Canadian, Vancouver's Andre Boudrias.

"He's going to be a good one," said Boudrias. "He works. He doesn't wait for the puck to come to him. And when he gets it, he can go."

A few weeks later the Sabres returned to Vancouver. This time the Canucks romped, 4-1 but the feeling was mutual about Gil. "He was held off the scoresheet," said Hal Sigurdson of the *Vancouver Sun,* "but the young center fairly reeks with talent. The Sabres were dangerous every time he stepped on the ice."

Perreault also was scoring goals; more goals than anybody else on the Sabres and when Buffalo occasionally would win a hockey game, the chances were that Gil played a part in it. By Christmas week 1970 he had accumulated 14 goals and on December 26th, the Sabres invaded Perreault's old stomping grounds, The Montreal Forum.

In that game the favored Canadiens grabbed a 3-0 lead in the first period and appeared certain to run away with

the game. But, with less than a minute remaining in the
opening period Perreault scored. At 12:00 of the second
period Serge Savard put Montreal ahead, 4-1 but once
again it was Perreault who narrowed the margin to 4-2
and Buffalo finally tied the game with two more goals in
the last period to come away with a 4-4 tie. "You don't
usually come back the way we did," enthused Imlach.

By now Perreault had skated against his erstwhile idol,
Beliveau, and, as they say in French-Canada, "Il gagne
ses epaulettes!"—he earned his medals!

"When I got on the ice," said Perreault, "I didn't even
think about Beliveau and I wasn't intimidated. If I started
being intimidated, I wouldn't play a good game, so nobody
is going to intimidate me easily."

One of the more fascinating questions of the season was
just how Imlach and Perreault would work together.
Punch came to Buffalo with the martinet's reputation of
not coddling players, including stars like Frank Mahovlich or potential stars such as Perreault. It is a reputation of
which Imlach is proud and he made no bones about it.

"Sure," Imlach explained "You can take a guy aside in
a bus or plane and tell him what ever you have to, to make
him play better; but in the locker room you can't make
exceptions. You gotta treat everybody the same. If the
guy is a sensitive type who can't take the harsh stuff, well,
that's life."

The word was that Punch couldn't work with young
players, and if anybody was young, chronologically at
least, it was Perreault. Yet, by mid-January 1971 Gil had
scored 17 goals and, lo and behold, the Sabres were
skating on the heels of the Detroit Red Wings and the
Canucks. Was Imlach a genius after all?

"Hockey is made up of two things," Punch said, "talent
the technical side—and intangibles such as desire, the will
to win, guts, and all that. I know we're going to be low on
talent for a while, but what we can have right away is the
intangibles. All we need is one good line . . . and we've got
this kid, Perreault."

Yes, he did, and on January 16th, the Sabres were
visiting the Metropolitan Sports Center in Bloomington,
Minnesota, to play the North Stars. The final score was

4-3 for Buffalo. Imlach got mileage out of his intangibles and the winning goal out of Gilbert Perreault.

"Gil will be a superstar as sure as I'm talking to you," said Charlie Barton, the hockey writer for the *Buffalo Courier-Express*. "His problem is that he's got nobody to play with. His right wing is Eddie Shack, who's really a left wing, and his left wing is Ron Anderson.

"They can't keep up with him. But can you imagine what he'd be doing if he had wingers like Bob Nevin and Vic Hadfield to skate with."

Gilbert Perreault, the human being, is a smiling young man who exudes an Englebert Humperdinck kind of sex appeal. The son of Ray Perreault, a French-Canadian railroad worker, Gil has three brothers and two sisters, all married. He is the youngest; the only single child in the family. He was born in Arthabaska (pop. 5,000), Quebec.

"I played my first hockey when I was around seven years old," said Perreault whose English is quite limited and very clipped with a French accent. "I played a lot with older fellows and when I was 16 I went to play for the Junior Canadiens. But first I played lower hockey."

Gil had been scouted by Phil Wimmer, manager of the Junior Canadiens, who assigned him to Thetford Mines in the Provincial Junior League in 1965. From there he progressed to the Junior Canadiens where he'd skate on the same Forum ice as Beliveau, often following the NHL ace onto the ice after the big Canadiens held a workout.

"Jean would try something in a practice," said Roger Bedard, who coached Perreault on the Junior Canadiens, "the the next thing you knew Gil would be trying the same move."

By no small coincidence, it was Imlach who coached Beliveau when Jean played for the Quebec Aces in his pre-NHL days. "Perreault is a faster skater than Beliveau ever was," said Imlach. "When Gil opens up he's really something to see."

While playing for the Junior Canadiens, Gil was confronted with the usual problem facing a talented young stickhandler—education or hockey. Some accept college scholarships, play more hockey and then, after they obtain a degree, move to the NHL. Others, like Bobby Orr, conveniently quit school, much to their parents' dismay.

Gil quit school after completing his 11th grade in Canada. "He was good at school," said his father, "but there comes the choice. Well, he was so good at hockey that he went that way and, of course, I am proud of him."

"I wouldn't want to put a jinx on him by comparing Gil to Beliveau," said Imlach, "so I wouldn't want to say he's the best since this guy or that guy."

But as the 1970-71 season concluded it became more and more apparent that Perreault not only would be the NHL's rookie of the year but, perhaps, the most outstanding rookie in league history. After all, the superb Beliveau scored only 13 goals in his first full NHL season, although the Canadiens' ace admittedly was hampered with injuries and was forced out of more than 25 games.

Perreault's lustre reached its shiniest hue during the 1971 All-Star Game at Boston. Both Gil and Bobby Orr of the Bruins were the stars of the contest and, from that point on, Perreault seemed to improve on his general excellence.

"I didn't play that well through December 1970," Perreault insisted. "I don't now why. Before Chistmas I didn't have good morale. After that I felt good in the head."

During a 16-game span in January 1971 he scored 13 goals and nine assists. By March he surpassed the 30-goal plateau and was taking dead aim on the rookie goal-scoring record of 34, not to mention the total point mark of 65.

Gil also admitted that his problem was part cerebral. He finished the season topping the former goal record—previously held by Nels Stewart—by four and the point mark by seven.

Even opposition coaches concerned with promoting their own rookies for awards had special endorsements for Perreault. Doug Barkley of the Detroit Red Wings allowed that he wanted his forward Tom Webster to win the Calder rookie Trophy but favored Gil.

Although New York Ranger goalie Gilles Villemure was also a hot candidate for rookie honors, general manager-coach Emile Francis went out of his way to laud Perreault. "The last time we played Buffalo," Francis recalled, "Gil went around our defense like a hoop around a barrel. This kind is so good there's no way to stop him if he's coming in one-on-one. No way. He has all the moves and he has great range."

Just how high Perreault will climb in years to come is entirely up to him. Those who know these things believe his horizons are limitless.

"All you need to know," wrote author John Miller in *The Canadian Magazine*, "is that most surveyors of the NHL farm system meat market agree that Perreault does wonderful things to their remembrances of rookies past— 'He's another Beliveau.' 'He's another Howe.' 'He's another Hull.' 'He's another Orr.'

"If they're right, Gil Perreault, two or three years from now, will be coming at us from all sorts of incredible directions."

He might even make some people forget—but just for a moment—the most exciting scorer of them all, Maurice "The Rocket" Richard.

DEREK SANDERSON *The most flamboyant, bizarre and unpredictable character in contemporary hockey is Derek Sanderson—and few will argue the point.*

He was the first of the modern stickhandlers to defy tradition by wearing a mustache; by openly criticizing Clarence Campbell, the president of the National Hockey League; and by dissecting a majority of his opponents in his own autobiography, "I've Got To Be Me."

In 1969 he startled the conservative hockey world by sporting a wardrobe of high-fashion mod clothes; by making it obvious that he likes the company of attractive

*women; and by telling the Boston Bruins management
that he would wear his hair as long as he pleased.*

*As the Bruins' center, Derek was relegated to the role
of third line defensive center yet he scored 29 goals and
34 assists for 63 points last season and got more publicity than teammate Phil Esposito who scored 76 goals and
76 assists.*

Sanderson was featured in such magazines as Life,
Esquire, Time *and* Sport. *He was the star of a recently-
completed full-length film, "Face-Off," and the subject of
a major Columbia Broadcasting System television profile.
He also appeared on TV as a guest with Dick Cavett,
Johnny Carson and Merv Griffin, plus his own TV gab
show on a Boston station.*

*Much has been written about Derek, yet few people—
particularly his teammates—really know him. In an effort
to gain a new insight into the Sanderson personality, this
author taped an interview with Ken "Hawk" Harrelson,
the colorful ex-baseball player-golfer, who was one of
Derek's few close friends the first season Sanderson came
to play the Bruins. The following is the first published tran-
scription of "Harrelson-on-Sanderson."*

I heard about Derek long before I met him. Having
played for the Boston Red Sox, it was only natural for me
to read about the Bruins. I noticed stories about the kid
called "Turk."

My attorney, Bob Woolf, told me that Sanderson came
up to his office. He said Turk was really something; that
he told Woolf he was going to be a big star and that he
(Woolf) should handle him. I wasn't a hockey fan at that
time, but I couldn't help being fascinated by Bob's description of him.

Then I met him. I couldn't get over how small he was.
His language was unbelievably profane, loaded with four-
letter words. He doesn't care who was there or what he
said. He's just plain crude, like a raw piece of ore you
might find in the earth. But you could also sense a pre-
cious stone. It was just a question of getting underneath
the surface.

I found out he was just a kid who had come up the hard
way; also that everything was going his way, he wasn't

going to let anything change his mind or habits. My impression was that Derek wasn't going to let anybody take it away from him.

More important, as far as I was concerned, was that I liked the guy and we quickly became good friends. When that happened, I decided that I wanted to help him in areas where I thought he could use it.

A friend of mine and I tried to persuade Derek to cut down his vulgar language. We'd sit down and discuss ways for talking with people and the proper methods of social behavior. This was strictly against his will and he rejected it. I've said this to his face and I'll say it here: I think Derek still has a lot of growing up to do. Occasionally, he has listened to me.

Once, we were out on a date and I could tell he was working hard not to use any vulgarity. He was trying all night not to be profane but, finally a word slipped out and at a very bad time and it made me mad. I jumped all over him about it and I knew he was sorry. It was the one time I've ever been really angry with him.

But this very brashness of his also is a strong quality. He's all male; and men like his frankness. I knew that all the guys on the Cleveland Indians were fascinated with Derek. When I went to spring training they all asked me about him. Every time he played, they'd find a clipping about him and bring it to me. They appreciate his honesty. He tells it like it is. If he doesn't like somebody, he says so. As a result, sometimes his honesty casts him in a bad light; people often don't want to hear the truth.

More important than that is his behavior in the rink. As far as I'm concerned he is among the top two or three colorful athletes in all professional sports today. He has a special charisma about him that makes him something like a demi-god.

I've had people say to me that when I went out to right field in Fenway Park there was a magnet toward right field and the rest of the park seemed to be shut off from the spectators. This is the kind of feeling I get in a hockey rink when Derek is on the ice. People's attention is drawn toward him; that long hair, that look of ferocity, that number 16.

His expression fascinates people because he never seems to change it. It's positively fierce, something like a gargoyle. Once you look at it, you can't take your eyes away from it. I've never seen an athlete in any sport command so much attention as Derek does when he hits the ice. He automatically becomes the focal point.

One reason for this is that fans sense the animal in him. When he gets angry it bursts forth. He's got a great capacity for rationalization, but he doesn't use it. He doesn't rationalize, he reacts. This is what makes him so exciting.

Our personalities are alike in many ways; the difference is that I'm a little more flexible in my behavior than he is. I think it'll take Derek a few more years before he acquires this flexibility. And, by that, I don't mean he'll change as a person so much as I think he'll refine the rough edges.

It didn't take me very long to discover that Derek is either loved or hated, depending on whom you're rooting for or which team you're playing with. One night I was sitting with Gordie Howe, talking hockey. All of a sudden Gordie said, "Sanderson's a good friend of your's, isn't he?" I said, "Yeah, he's a good friend. He's a helluva good kid."

Howe looked at me for a second, then sneered, "Yeah, that little——." That bothered me. I said, 'Gordie, do me a favor, take it easy." He said, "yeah, I'll take it easy. I'll put about 20 stitches in his face." But, if you ask Gordie whether he'd like to have Derek playing for the Red Wings, he'd jump up and down trying to get him.

Needless to say, the more I got to know Derek, the more I became a dyed-in-the-wool hockey fan. Every time I'd see Derek play I'd say to myself, "If there's another life here on earth I'd love to come back as a hockey player. If I had to do it all over again I'd love to be born American, go to Canada, learn to play hockey and then come back here just like Derek; not like Bobby Orr."

That might sound a little strange, considering Bobby Orr is the greatest player in the world. He's fantastic, exciting and all that but Derek is *the most exciting* player in the game. To understand the difference, put it in baseball terms.

It's like the contrast between Mickey Mantle and Joe Pepitone. In this case, Orr would be Mantle and Sanderson would be Pepitone. If you wanted to enjoy the game, you watched Mantle. He was beautiful to watch. But if you wanted to enjoy the game *and* have some fun, you watched Pepitone. Like Mantle, Orr is a great machine. But Derek has both ability and the flamboyancy.

Of all the ball players in the majors , Pete Rose reminds me most of Derek in athletic style. Rose is reckless and exciting. In football, Dick Butkus has the same kind of magnetism. When he hits the field everybody's eyes are riveted on Butkus.

Unfortunately, Derek's flamboyance tends to overshadow the fact that he's a very talented hockey player. He's the only guy on the Bruins—and that includes Bobby Orr—who's never played a bad game when I was watching. A great game for another hockey player is just a normal one for Derek. I believe that before his career is over he'll have done more for hockey than anybody in the game because of the combination of his ability *and* personality.

I realize that I'm bypassing Bobby Orr in this comparison and, remember, Orr is a good friend of mine. He's one of the nicest people I've met, but I'll explain what I mean about his magnetism compared with Derek's. I had a possible deal to open a restaurant in Boston and the backer asked me if I'd consider having Bobby go in with me as a partner. I said, "No, I'd rather have Derek Sanderson."

He was a little surprised until I explained that Derek would be a bigger asset than Bobby. First of all, Derek has that tremendous sex appeal and, besides that, he has a tremendous instinct for promotion, which Orr lacks. Derek would go on nationwide television and promote his place while Bobby would be a little reluctant. Right now I think Derek is a bigger drawing card in the Boston area than Orr is, although Bobby is bigger on a national scale.

Derek and I have a number of discussions about our games. We agreed that the mental aspect is the most important one in both sports. I think baseball is 95 per cent mental and five percent physical, once you've proven you've got the ability. Derek said the mental aspect is just as strong in hockey.

When he's not in the mood to fight, he just won't because he knows he's going to lose. Lots of times the two of us get together and daydream like a pair of kids. We set up situations about how we'd like to be and what we'd like to do. When we come out of it we both feel a lot better.

Every so often I think I see a touch of Denny McLain in Derek. Like Denny, Derek is the kind of person who leaps without looking. For example, he'll sign a paper and then, two days later, he'll call his attorney, Bob Woolf and say, "Bobby, what did I sign?" He'll sign a blank piece of paper to acquire a car, then send it to Bobby, and ask, "Bobby, how much is it going to cost me?" If he sees something he likes, he gets it.

That shouldn't be too much of a disadvantage to him in years to come, because he's one of the rare athletes whose personality and good-looks will enable him to make more money off the ice than he will on it. In a few years he's going to be one of the four or five highest-paid hockey players.

I have a positive influence over him in fashion. We both wear clothes well. Derek can wear anything, absolutely anything, and look good in it. Every so often I'll go shopping and I'll buy something, such as a tie, and while I'm buying it I'll actually be buying it for Derek because I know he'll love it.

Some people suggested that I'm jealous of Derek's popularity but that's not true at all. I feel like his big brother. When he plays a good game I know I enjoy it more than he does. I've had a lot of thrills in my career. I've played in a World Series, was Player of the Year one season. Yet, considering all of this, I get the greatest thrill and satisfaction in watching Derek do well.

When he gets into a fight I become angry at the guy he's fighting. If somebody hits him I get mad. This happened one night after I had broken my leg. I was in the hospital watching the Rangers and Bruins in the Stanley

Cup playoffs on television. My leg had just been operated on and I had to be as stationary as possible.

My leg was propped up so that it wouldn't swell and the cast had just been put on it. All of a sudden I noticed that Derek was involved in a fight with a couple of Rangers. Well, two minutes after that fight was over my leg had blown up something awful. My leg was blue, my toes were blue and I was sitting there—along with my mother who had been visiting me—pounding the bed because of what those Rangers had done to Derek. I was so excited my leg was aching.

I remembered that Billy Fairbairn of the Rangers sucker-punched Derek. That burned me up so much I made up my mind that if I ever run into him I'm definitely going to provoke him. I just don't like him for what he did to Derek. And I don't like Walt Tkaczuk and Dave Balon, who played on the line with Fairbairn. They're probably the nicest guys in the world, but just because of what they did to Derek I can't stand them.

Not that Derek can't take care of himself; he can. I relate to him as if he's my little brother and I don't want anybody to touch him. When I was traded to Cleveland I gave Derek my apartment in Boston; and I know that he'd do the same for me. When I was in the hospital he paid me several visits. A reporter asked me if Derek was the second Hawk Harrelson. "At the moment," I told him, "you'd have to say that I am the old Sanderson."

Derek has a good mind, but he doesn't use it all the time. He's not as smart or as sophisticated as I am. But once he mellows, he'll be almost the same way I am now—still a character, still Peck's Bad Boy of Hockey.

I'm just glad the Boston Bruins have him because I love Boston and I want Boston teams to excel. I think the Bruins are the greatest thing in the world for hockey. They have the supermen—Orr, Phil Esposito—but without Derek, they're just sad skunks.

GARRY UNGER There are many ways to enter the National Hockey League, but Garry Unger took an unusual route in the autumn of 1967. The speedy blond center was 19 years old at the time and eligible to play another season of Junior hockey with the London, Ontario, Nationals, then a farm team of the Toronto Maple Leafs.

A few days before the start of training camp Unger suffered a knee injury. He visited Toronto for treatment and, while there, was invited to scrimmage with the NHL club. Just then, Maple Leaf forward Frank Mahovlich was hospitalized. Someone was needed to fill the void and Unger got the call.

After playing 15 games, he wanted to go back to the minors for more experience, and general manager-coach Punch Imlach agreed. But before the season ended Garry was dispatched to the Detroit Red Wings along with Frank Mahovlich and Peter Stemkowski for Norm Ullman, Paul Henderson and Floyd Smith as well as the rights to Carl Brewer. It was one of the biggest deals in hockey history.

Unger reacted to the switch like a prisoner being released from jail. "The best part," he said, "is the lack of pressure in Detroit. When I was in Toronto the pressure almost smothered me. I never had a feeling of belonging there. Management bugged me. If you made an honest mistake on the ice it was the same as committing a crime. Pretty soon you lost confidence in yourself and when that happens you're really in trouble."

In his first 13 games as a Red Wing near the end of the 1967-68 season Unger averaged better than a point per game. "There's nothing he can't do," said Gordie Howe, Detroit's father figure, "shoot, check and make the plays. And when you tell him something, he listens—that's rare these days. Besides, he's aggressive more aggressive than anyone I've played with recently."

Typical of Unger's versatility was a goal he scored against the Boston Bruins. Using his stick as a harpoon, he jabbed the puck away from defenseman Dallas Smith and spurted around the Bruin along the right boards. The puck now was on his right side, the backhand. Despite the difficult angle, Unger managed to hurl the puck past goalie Gerry Cheevers.

"Garry was a real pro on that play," said Howe. "He showed me about four moves on one play. He gave Smith a little change of pace—something you don't expect from a youngster. Then, he made a helluva play to get the goal."

Unger scored 24 goals and 20 assists in 1968-69, his first full season. A year later, with 42 goals and 24 assists, he was considered a Red Wing leader. Then, the roof fell in.

Prior to the start of the 1970-71 training camp Ned Harkness, former Cornell University hockey coach, was named the new bench coach in Detroit. By this time Garry was wearing his hair like a rock star. When Unger checked into the Red Wings' training camp Harkness blanched at the sight of his blond center and ordered him to trim the golden locks. Unger complied, but not enough to suit Harkness.

He made Garry return to the barber shop three times before the coiffure was acceptable. By this time an air of hostility flowed between Unger and Harkness.

"In my opinion," Unger said, "the length of my hair was irrelevant to hockey. Far more important was the fact that I slipped on a diving board in September and injured my back."

Unger suffered a scoring drought from the beginning of the season. He blamed his injury, plus Harkness' request that a player skate hard almost every minute he's on the ice.

"He thinks if you're not skating, you're not working," said Unger. "You can do it for 30 games in college hockey, but you can't do it for 80 in the NHL. I tried that hard-skating technique a few years ago and by February, I was finished. I just didn't have it anymore."

After 34 games Unger scored only nine goals and the Red Wings were languishing near the bottom of the East Division. Then Detroit owner Bruce Norris dramatically named Harkness as manager and appointed Doug Barkley as coach. Shortly thereafter, Unger was dispatched to St. Louis along with Wayne Connolly for Red Berenson and Tim Ecclestone.

"I hated to part with him," said Harkness. "But Unger wasn't doing anything. He was going downhill more than uphill."

By contrast, the St. Louis front office was delighted with the move. "We got a hockey player with a great future in Unger," said then Blues manager, Scotty Bowman.

In one of his first turns on the ice for St. Louis, Garry lost the puck and the enemy scored. It was the type of blunder which could have upset a less dynamic athlete, but he fought back. In a matter of weeks he captured the hearts of St. Louis rooters who so passionately cheered Berenson in bygone days. The reason was simple—Unger was playing the brand of hockey that brought him 42 goals two seasons ago.

"Garry convinced me he should be a 40-plus scorer every year," said Bowman.

Unger agreed. "I look at some guys," he said, "and notice how they sweat and slave to get the job done. But scoring comes easy to me. Even as a kid I could score goals. I just have this gift, and thank God for it."

A non-smoker and non-drinker, Unger nevertheless has been fitted into the Derek Sanderson "swinger" category because of his penchant for dating women like Pam Eldred, the former Miss America, his more than 200 fan letters per week, and his unusual business dealings.

"Just before I was traded by the Wings," said Garry, "I bought 11 prime acres outside Detroit. The idea was to raise quarter horses on a ranch and help pay for them through a riding stable. Already the value of the land has increased enough to make me stay with the plan as a sound investment."

Likewise, the St. Louis Blues are convinced that landing Unger was one of the best long-range investments ever made by the West Division team.

LORNE "GUMP" WORSLEY Last February 7th an exhausted butterball of a man leaned back on his bench in the bowels of Boston Garden and smiled. "The way I played tonight," said Minnesota North Stars goalie Gump Worsley, "I must have made the oldtimers feel good."

The 41-year-old Worsley, ancient by National Hockey League standards, had just made 63 saves against the Bruins to provide Minnesota with a tie. The North Stars should have been defeated.

"I've never seen a better job of goaltending by anyone," said Bruins goalie Ed Johnston. "I certainly haven't seen Gump play a better game."

The last of the veteran goaltenders to play without a protective face mask, Worsley was a prime reason why the North Stars were able to reach the Stanley Cup semi-finals before bowing in six games to the world champion Montreal Canadiens.

A throwback to an earlier hockey era, the 5-7, 180 pound Worsley has no illusions about his ability to play a 70 game season, the way he did in 1955-56 for the New York Rangers. "A goalie can't go the entire route these days," said Worsley. "The schedule is too long and the puck is coming at you too fast. You show me a goalie who plays every game and I'll show you a guy who'll be swinging from a tree by the time the season's over."

It was over a decade ago that Worsley realized fully the dangers of goaltending. In December 1960 a shot ricocheted off a stick like a bullet hitting a rock and struck Gump in the left eye. He was taken to the dressing room where the doctor told him he was lucky. He was cut above and below the eye but he wasn't blinded; at least not permanently.

His manager, Muzz Patrick, asked Gump if he could continue. Worsley nodded. He had a 2-0 lead in the first period. When the game had ended he had a 5-2 lead. But he didn't see out of the left eye until a day later.

"Going back on the ice was the craziest thing I've ever done," Worsley said later. Then he paused and grinned that impish grin of his and added, "But you've got to be crazy to be a goalie."

For ten more years the man who looks like a bloated fire hydrant blocked National Hockey League shots. In time he was traded from New York to his native Montreal. Playing for the Canadiens, he helped the Flying Frenchmen to a few Stanley Cups and clearly established himself as one of the supreme—if not most unlikely-looking—goaltenders big-league hockey has known. He loved being a hero in his own home town.

"When I retire," he said, "it'll be because I can't help this club anymore."

Not long after that the Canadiens fired him.

No, it wasn't the usual kind of firing. It never is in sports. Worsley helped the Canadiens to the Stanley Cup in 1969 and he expected to do the same in 1970. He played 34 games—not bad for a man past 40—and he had played them well.

Rogatien Vachon, Worsley's younger alter-ego in the Montreal net, also played well. But the French-Canadian Vachon still lacked Worsley's *savoire-faire*.

At the very least Worsley expected to divide the goaltending evenly with Vachon in 1969-70. But the Canadiens' coach, Claude Ruel, was feeling a bit heady over winning the Stanley Cup. When the season began Ruel decided on Vachon as his goaltender and Worsley as a bench decoration. Communications between Gump and Ruel became nonexistant.

"We never spoke," Worsley remarked. "How can you get along with a guy you never talk to?"

In December 1969 after a long and unsuccessful run with Vachon, Ruel listed Gump as his starting goalie for a game in Pittsburgh. Gump shook his head. No good. The assignment on the bench had left him ill-equipped to rush into a game. "I haven't practiced enough," he said.

It was then that Worsley was fired.

The firing, in this case, was something along the lines of the Chinese Water Torture. The Montreal general manager Sam Pollock told Gump he was being sent to the American Hockey League. He would get himself in shape by playing for Les Voyageurs. This was like telling the president of the United States he should brush up on the constitution by returning to law school for a few months. The Gump told Pollock to bugger-off.

"I had told Sam even before the season that I was interested only in playing for the Canadiens and that I wouldn't play anywhere else. Especially not in the minors."

"We want you to play for the Canadiens," said Pollock, "but first you'll have to play for the Voyageurs."

"In that case," snapped Worsley, "I won't play at all."

The Gump's declaration of independence did not come as easily as it sounded. At age 40, there aren't many jobs open to a portly goaltender who crossed the boss. There was a wife—a delightful woman, Doreen—and four children to support. All he needed was for the wife to get upset about his decision and he'd be miserable for the rest of his life.

"Whaddya' think?" Gump asked Doreen, who has been married to him since he entered the NHL. Before she opened her mouth he knew the answer.

Worsley laughed when he told me what she replied. "She said, 'Tell them to jam it. You'll get something; don't worry about that.' Those were her exact words."

With captain Jean Beliveau and left wing John Ferguson ailing, the Canadiens were in trouble. Pollock and Ruel could feel the pressure. They had to defend their move while simultaneously angling to lure Worsley back to the team.

The press was told that Gump had been out of shape and was uninterested during practices. "Imagine that," said Worsley in retrospect. "They said I didn't practice enough. What are they talkin' about? I've played that way all my life, for Phil Watson of the Rangers and Toe Blake on the Canadiens."

Pollock knew that he couldn't establish a dialogue between Ruel and Worsley. He needed a go-between respected by both sides. He went to ex-coach Blake, the Canadiens' minister-without-portfolio and asked him to talk to Worsley. Blake said that he would.

"Blake came to me," Gump recalled, "and brought up the business about my practicing. I said, 'Toe you know I never worked hard in practice. That's nothing new.' He agreed. Then, when he left me he said, 'Well, I did my job; I talked to you'."

Support kept mounting for Worsley. Hall of Famer, Maurice "Rocket" Richard, writes a weekly sports column in a French-Canadian paper, Dimanche-Matin. Early in the season Richard observed that the Canadiens were erring in not playing Worsley. He underlined his point when the Gump walked out. "The Rocket ripped the ship out of them," said Gump.

Seemingly adrift without a life-saver at first, Worsley suddenly found himself surrounded by helpers. "Punch Imlach told me to my face that he'd grab me for his expansion team wherever he was," said Gump. "That made me feel better but, still, I would have liked to finish my career in Montreal, my home."

When Blake's mission failed, the Canadien's lost their last chance of persuading Worsley to return—under the Forum's conditions. But if management would relent, then Gump would come back. The Canadiens now had Vachon as number one goaltender and Phil Myre, a tall blond French-Canadian as Worsley's replacement. Myre had never played in the NHL before, but that didn't matter as much as the fact that Vachon was top banana. Some people figured that was not good for either Vachon or the Canadiens. Gump was one of those people.

"Roggie was a good goaltender," Worlsey told me, "but he's like other goaltenders; he needs somebody behind him on the bench to keep him on his toes. Maybe Myre wasn't quite ready at the time and Roggie started thinking "what do I have to worry about"?"

By the end of January Pollock had to make a decision

either back Ruel to the hilt or get a replacement and bring back Worsley. Pollock went with Ruel and opened negotiations with Wren Blair of Minnesota to deal Gump to the North Stars. If Worsley was angry at Pollock for prior treatment he received, he was even more furious over the manner in which he learned he was traded to the North Stars. He heard about it on the radio.

Heading for the North Stars in February 1970 was like being sent on a rescue boat to help The Titanic. Minnesota was sinking in the quicksand of an endless losing streak that threatened to shut the club out of the playoffs. Optimism was non-existent.

The desperate Minnesotans looked to Worsley to save them. Somehow, somewhere, he was quoted as saying, he'd lead them to the holy grail. It was not quite accurate. "I didn't say I'd make sure Minnesota would be in the playoffs," Worsley remembered. "I was misquoted. I said I'd do everything possible to help them make it."

North Star coach Charlie Burns made it clear he didn't expect any miracles from Worsley. "He told me to go into the dressing room and say what I wanted to say. They hadn't won in so long that nobody wanted the puck. They'd come off the bench and sit there like wooden indians. The first thing I did was talk to them. Next thing I knew they went up against Toronto and won, 8-0. I was on the bench and everytime it got quiet I'd get up and start cheering and yelling. They never had a guy like that before.

"When they were down a goal they'd get upset. I told them that in the NHL if you're down a goal you've got lots of time to get it back. All of a sudden we started to win. But what surprised me was that after only two practices they asked me to play."

On Saturday night, March 14th, 1970 Worsley was in the nets, beating Pittsburgh. On Sunday, Burns asked him to play again, this time in Madison Square Garden against New York. It was a difficult request because Worsely did not care for back-to-back assignments at his age. "Charlie asked me to play as long as I could," Gump said. "I figured I'd give it a try."

It was a memorable effort. The Gump exploited every

resource at his command, both mental and physical. Over-whelmed by the onrushing Rangers, the North Stars nevertheless held fast as Worsley blunted the New York attack. A goal by Ray Cullen late in the game put Minnesota ahead.

If the often-cynical Gump calls it "one of the better games in my career," it had to have been an NHL classic. More important to the North Stars it gave them the momentum to challenge the faltering Philadelphia Flyers for a playoff berth. On Saturday afternoon, April 4th, the Flyers played their final home game of the season. All they needed was a tie against the North Stars—as it turned out, all they needed was a goal—to win a playoff berth.

Gump Worsley did not allow the Flyers one goal. At 7:48 of the third period, defenseman Barry Gibbs of the North Stars lifted a Texas League shot into the Philadelphia end of the rink. It was the kind of shot that amateur goalies are supposed to stop but it bounced past Barnie Parent and the Flyers lost the game, 1-0.

"That's hockey," explained Worsley. "This game is strange. Things happen that you can't believe."

Take Gump Worsley as an example.

FLASHBACK

HOCKEY'S GREATEST COMEBACK

THERE ARE many comebacks in sports, but as far as the
National Hockey League is concerned there is absolutely
no question that *the comeback of all time* was engineered
by the Toronto Maple Leafs in the spring of 1942.

In that era the rivalry between the Leafs and Detroit
Red Wings was so hot that battles between players and
officials were more the rule than the exception. The first
big fight occurred in the 1940 Stanley Cup series, when
every player on both teams joined a brawl that produced
seventeen $25 fines. After that, Hap Day, the Leafs' coach,
denounced the Wings as "a bunch of hoodlums," an alle-
gation that provoked Detroit Manager Jack Adams to
reply: "We're just sorry we can't play the Leafs seven
nights in a row."

By the time the Toronto and Detroit teams met in the
Stanley Cup finals of April 1942, the enmity between
them had reached a new high. That year the Leafs, a
well-balanced club led by high-scoring Gordie Drillon and
Syl Apps, finished second in the regular season race, 15
points ahead of the fifth-place Red Wings. In the playoffs
the Wings beat Montreal and Boston, qualifying to meet
Toronto, which had defeated league-leading New York in
the other semifinal.

"We may not have the greatest hockey club in the
world," said Adams, on the eve of the opening game at
Maple Leaf Gardens in Toronto, "but we're loaded with
fighting heart."

Despite Adams' optimism, the Leafs were considered
8-5 favorites to win their first Stanley Cup since 1932. The
odds looked good until the opening period of the first
game, when Detroit scored twice, submitting the classier
Leafs to brutal physical punishment in the process. "The
rugged visitors ripped the Toronto defense into ribbons

with heavy bodychecks," was the way the Associated Press described it.

So relentless were the Detroit skaters that when Jimmy Orlando, the rough Red Wings' defenseman, slashed Toronto rookie Bob Goldham and received a major penalty, the Leafs' power play was held to only one shot on goal by the Red Wing's penalty killers.

Toronto fought back to tie the score 2-2, but Don Grosso, the Wings' leading scorer, finally won the game for Detroit. Rebounding from a terrific body check by Bingo Kampman, he fired a high shot to beat Toronto Goalie Turk Broda at 14:11 of the second period.

The surprise in the Leafs' dressing room after the first loss was converted to numbness after the second contest at Toronto, which was virtually a carbon copy of the first. Employing their new and startling tactics to advantage, the Wings triumphed 4-2 as Grosso scored twice and tied a league record of eight Stanley Cup goals.

"Detroit's style had us buffaloed," explained Day. "That was the first time any club ever shot the puck into the end zone and flooded in after it. There was no center red line then, and the Detroits would simply get the puck across their own blue line and let it go into our end. Then they'd race in and get to it before we did."

Obviously shaken, Day was tempted to make lineup changes when the series moved to Detroit for the third and fourth games. He held off, hopeful that his aces—Drillon, Apps and Lorne Carr—would respond. Carr scored twice in the first period of the third game, but Jerry Brown and Joe Carvath matched them for the Wings.

Toronto appeared to gain an advantage when Detroit's firstline center, Sid Abel, left the game with a fractured jaw and was replaced by rookie Pat McReavy. But McReavy came through strong and scored the deciding goal in the third period, inspiring Detroit to a 5-2 victory.

Behind now three games to none and well aware that no hockey team had ever recovered to win four straight Stanley Cup games, Day was vilified by Toronto fans wherever he turned. "The abuse fell like rain," he recalled. "We got blasted in the papers and on the streets. Everywhere!"

Maple Leaf Gardens' directors demanded an explanation of the collapse. "I told them about Detroit's style," said Day. "And I told them our star defenseman, Bucko McDonald, was simply tired out. He had played wonderful hockey for us, but he was just tuckered out and couldn't cope with Detroit's shooting tactics. I said the same thing about Drillon. He was a great scorer but his style wasn't suited to that shoot-and-skate stuff."

"O.K.," said Colonel W.A.H. MacBrien, one of the Leafs' directors, when Day completed his explanation. "Now what are we going to do about it?"

Anticipating the question, Day then made the decision that was to launch the most amazing comeback in hockey annals. He recommended that veterans Drillon and McDonald be replaced by two rookies, right wing Don Metz, brother of regular left wing Nick Metz, and defenseman Ernie Dickens. Don Metz scored only two goals all season for Toronto, while Dickens played in just 10 NHL games. "We also decided to change our style and play the same type of hockey the Wings were using," said Day. "We figured that might stop 'em."

Day's revised lineup was regarded as insignificant. The consensus among writers covering the series was that Detroit was now unbeatable. So nobody took Billy Taylor seriously when the young Leafs' center discussed the series with Toronto newspaperman on the eve of the fourth game.

"Don't worry about us," said Taylor. "We'll take 'em four straight!" Well, four straight was how it had to be, that or nothing.

By the middle of the fourth game Taylor's boast was looking pretty frail. The Leafs seemed about finished. Mud Brunenteau and Abel had scored for Detroit while Wing Goaltender Johnny Mowers held Toronto scoreless. Then Bob Davidson broke the shutout at 13:54 of the second period, and Carr flicked in a Taylor rebound to tie the score before the period ended and things began to look better for Toronto.

The Olympia Stadium's largest hockey crowd, 13,695,

rocked the arena at 4:18 of the third period when Carl Liscombe put Detroit ahead again 3-2. "They were awaiting the kill of the mighty Leafs," wrote Vern DeGeer, sports editor of the Toronto *Globe and Mail*.

Then, all of a sudden, the Leafs reawakened. Captain Apps, who had gone without a goal in the final series, slapped in a goal of his own at 8:15, and at 12:45 he fed Nick Metz a pass which gave Toronto the winning score. "As the game ended," wrote DeGeer, "Grosso and Eddie Wares of the Wings became embroiled in a heated argument with Referee Mel Harwood. They drew $50 and $25 fines. Then Manager Adams rushed across the ice to the penalty box and traded blows with Harwood. NHL President Frank Calder became involved when he left his box to get the referee's report on the incident. Spectators joined in the battle before police could separate them. Both Harwood and President Calder needed a police escort to escape safely from the building."

Late that evening President Calder announced the indefinite suspension of Adams and forbade him from any further bench management of the Wings during the series. Wares and Grosso were fined $100 each by Calder for their participation in the brawl. Ebbie Goodfellow became the Wings player-coach.

When the teams returned to Toronto for the fifth game, Don Metz was named the permanent replacement for Drillon on a line with Apps and Nick Metz, while Dickens was called upon to take a full turn on defense substituting for McDonald. Back at Maple Leaf Gardens, Day gathered his team in the dressing room and pointed to the inscription painted on the wall: *DEFEAT DOES NOT REST LIGHTLY ON OUR SHOULDERS*. Minutes later, on the ice, the Leafs were irrepressible as they subdued Detroit 9-3. Don Metz led the Toronto attack with three goals and two assists, while Apps scored twice and assisted on three others.

Now the Wings were reeling. Goodfellow ordered a shake-up for the sixth game in Detroit, summoning Gus Giesebrecht, Joe Fisher and Doug McCaig from their Indianapolis farm team to replace Eddie Bush, Pat McReavy and Adam Brown. But none of the Wings could contain Don Metz. After 14 seconds of the second period, he intercepted a pass near the Detroit goal and beat Mowers with a quick shot. It was his fourth goal in three games. Bob Goldham and Billy Taylor added goals in the last period to give Toronto a 3-0 victory and a 3-3 tie in the playoffs.

"By the time the seventh and deciding game rolled around," said DeGeer, "so much pent-up enthusiasm had attached itself to the series that the teams attracted 16,-218 customers to the final match, the largest crowd to see a hockey game in Canada."

After a scoreless first period, Syd Howe put Detroit ahead with a backhand shot at 1:44 of the second period. Sensing victory, the Wings tightened their defense and preserved the lead through the second period and early minutes of the third. But their carefully laid defensive plans were disrupted when Orlando received a two-minute tripping penalty in the fifth minute of the final period.

Desperately, the Wings battled the clock and seemed to have successfully killed the penalty as Orlando stepped out of the box. But Toronto's Carr had possession of the puck at the blue line and fed it ahead to Taylor, who feinted a shot and passed to Dave Schriner. His shot skimmed tantalizingly across the ice just out of Mowers' reach and into the net.

Less than two minutes later Johnny McCreedy of Toronto was checked as he skated in the Detroit zone. The puck flew crazily in the air and landed at the mouth of the Red Wings' goal. Little Pete Langelle, who was stationed near the crease awaiting a pass, took a swipe and Toronto ahead 2-1.

The stunned Wings threw five men into Toronto territory in an effort to pull even, but their tactics backfired when Carr knocked Howe to the ice and fed the puck to Taylor, the kid who earlier had promised four straight wins. Taylor shot the puck to Schriner, who scored at 16:13 of the period. For the next three minutes and 47 seconds the Leafs held fast and won the game 3-1—and the Stanley Cup.

Toronto's unprecedented effort was voted "The Comeback of the Half Century" by Canadian sportswriters. "No matter what the future holds," said Hap Day, "there'll never be an experience like this one."

Postscript: Day almost had to eat his words three years later. In the 1945 Stanley Cup final round between Detroit and Toronto, the Maple Leafs won the first three games, whereupon the Red Wings came back to win the next three. But Toronto defeated Detroit 2-1 in the seventh and final games at Detroit.

SPECIAL BONUS SECTION

THE MONTREAL MYSTIQUE

"MINE honor," wrote William Shakespeare in *King Richard II,* "is my life; both grow in one; Take honor from me, and my life is done."

In an era when honor and tradition are easily dismissed, when 50-goal seasons became as meaningful as Confederate dollar bills—one hockey team constantly rekindles a special mystique.

The Montreal Canadiens, "The Flying Frenchmen," are the oldest team in the National Hockey League. The organization is cloaked in an aura of mysticism bordering on the supernatural.

Thus, when the Canadiens swoop from behind—as they did in the classic 1971 Stanley Cup series with Boston and Chicago—and soar to victory, it is hailed as more than a mortal victory. It was inspired by the memories of revered former Montreal aces such as Billy Boucher, George Hainsworth, Sylvio Mantha, Howie Morenz and Maurice "Rocket" Richard. The manner in which the Canadiens won the 1971 Stanley Cup revives these memories.

"Pride," shouted Peter Mahovlich, a splendid performer for the Canadiens in the playoffs, "nothing but pride got us the Cup."

Before Peter Mahovlich became a Canadien he played for the Detroit Red Wings, and those associated with him then say that pride was not a part of his constitution. Laughs, yes; pride no.

But, John Ferguson, the Montreal left wing who for years oozed with the honor of representing Montreal and wearing the bleu (blue), blanc (white) and rouge (red) uniform got hold of Peter.

"Ferguson," says rookie goalie Ken Dryden, "can wither you with a look."

But Fergie did more than look. He had been with the

Canadiens for years and he knew what the Montreal mystique was all about. He gave Peter a few lessons while they were teaching at a hockey school in the summer of 1970.

"I told him to get mad," says Ferguson, "and start leaning on people. You gotta hate those other guys. He got the message."

Different Canadiens interpret the mystique in different ways. To defenseman Terry Harper the defeat of the big bad Bruins in April 1971 was not rooted in any one game, although many observers point to the come-from-behind triumph in the second match of the series.

"There was no turning point," said Harper, who had predicted the Canadiens victory all along, "we all wanted to win."

To Senator Hartland Molson, head of the family which owns the Montreal club, the Canadiens suggest more than simply a hockey team: they carry the spirit of French-speaking Quebec province.

"This club," Senator Molson once said, "is more than a professional sports organization. It's an institution, a way of life."

Defining this "way of life" is easy, it just depends on which *Quebecois* you ask. "We are not only a civilized race," a Laval University priest-historian once explained, "we are pioneers of civilization."

If the cleric suffered from slight delusions of grandeur, so then, have the Montreal Canadiens. But is this necessarily bad? Not necessarily.

"You have to believe that you're the best," says Peter Desbarats, a Montreal author and broadcaster. "Attitude is everything."

Anyone who has ever visited The Forum in Montreal emerges convinced that the attitude of the Canadiens' fan is something special: even in the 1969-70 season, the year of defeat.

"Sustained by the feeling that the great days will return," said an observer in *The Canadian Magazine*, "the Montreal fans came out—not to sit on their hands and coolly assess the play as do Toronto Maple Leaf fans, but to yell and cheer and coax their heroes forward to another era of glory."

The Canadiens were born in December 1909. Less than two years later the "French fact" that has long since been Montreal's trademark became evident when the National Hockey Association—later to become the NHL—ruled that the Canadiens were to sign only French-speaking players.

It took six years for *Les Canadiens* to win their first Stanley Cup. They played the Portland Rosebuds of the Pacific Coast Hockey Association in a best-of-five series which went the pulsating limit. Typical of what was to come again and again over the years, the Canadiens rallied late in the game, winning 2-1.

The Montreal heroes were already numerous. Up front there was Newsy Lalonde, a superb skater and scorer; and in the rear, guarding the nets, was George Vezina, after whom the goaltending trophy is named.

Nicknamed "The Chicoutimi Cucumber" because of his implacable facade, Vezina remained in the Canadiens nets through the early Twenties and led Montreal to another Cup victory in the Spring of 1924 although his lean body already was riddled by tuberculosis.

Nevertheless, he continued playing until the night of November 28, 1925 when he skated onto the ice at Mount Royal Arena to face Pittsburgh. His body temperature had climbed to 105 degrees, but he played the first period and was on the ice to start the second when, suddenly, the 6,000 spectators gasped as Vezina collapsed on the ice. He was carried out of the rink, never to play hockey again. Vezina died on March 24, 1926.

Curiously, before he died, Vezina actually designated his successor after watching George Hainsworth tend goal for Kitchener. Vezina advised Montreal boss Leo Dandaurand to hire him and soon Hainsworth became a winner of the Vezina Trophy.

But the new Canadiens hero was Howie Morenz, a forward whose speed was unmatched in the NHL. Alternately called "the Stratford Streak" and the "Mitchell Meteor"—he was brought up near those Ontario commu-

Once Richard retired, the princely Beliveau inherited the captaincy and remained the Canadiens' leader 'til last spring. The Montrealers won three more Cups for Blake in 1965, 1966 and 1968 when Toe finally retired. He was replaced by Claude Ruel who promptly won another Cup for the Canadiens.

Ruel's stewardship produced conflicts, causing manager Sam Pollock to trade goalie Gump Worsley in the middle of the 1969-70 season. After Montreal finished out of the playoffs, Pollock traded defenseman Ted Harris; but the grumbling continued. Both John Ferguson and Ralph Backstrom retired, ostensibly because of Ruel. While the season still was young Ruel was replaced by his assistant, Al MacNeil.

When Backstrom returned he was dealt to Los Angeles. Ferguson made his way back to the lineup and, once again, became the team catalyst. He retired last spring.

"They talk about Beliveau being the inspiration," says Boston center Derek Sanderson, "but the real drive for that team came from Ferguson. He was something else."

Derek is mostly right. The Canadiens finished third during the past season and were regarded as sacrificial lambs for the fearsome Bruins. Boston won the opening game and led the second match, 5-1, when Beliveau and Ferguson and friends reversed the trend, winning 7-5.

"We don't quit," snapped Ferguson. "This is a proud outfit." It remains to be seen if the Montreal mystique now holds up without Beliveau and Ferguson.

WHAT'S BEHIND HOCKEY VIOLENCE?

A VISITOR from outer space would have been puzzled had he crash-landed in Madison Square Garden during the second game of the New York-Toronto Stanley Cup playoff series last April.

Players from each team were sprinkled across the ice,

holding each other by the jersey or jabbing a fist into the enemy's jaw. At one point, Ed Giacomin, the Ranger's goaltender, sprinted 180 feet across the rink to tackle Jacques Plante.

The world series of hockey appeared to be nothing more than a pier six brawl with no holds barred. From St. Catherine's, Ontario, to St. Louis, Missouri, from the National Hockey League to the amateur Ontario Hockey Association brawls have made hockey look like boxing and wrestling exhibitions.

At times it was funny, like the night Rangers' defenseman Brad Park wrapped his arms around referee Lloyd Gilmour and pleaded with him not to get angry. Other times it was not only grim, but downright gory. Perhaps the following vignette will begin to explain the reasons for violence in hockey:

Pat Quinn, a Vancouver Canucks defenseman was happy. There he stood, 215 pounds of him wrapped in 20 pounds of protective armor, a joyous, murderous gleam in his eyes. The source of this delight was Danny Lawson of Minnesota, who was speeding down the ice, eyes riveted to the black puck gliding before the blade of his stick.

"I lie awake nights just thinking about a chance to throw a body check at somebody with his head down like that," Quinn said with a gap-toothed grin. He met Lawson solidly, halfway to nowhere. Lawson's face slammed into Quinn's rocklike elbow guard. Bloodstained teeth rattled across the ice as Lawson's jaw crumpled.

It's a bloody game, so bloody that the NHL estimates at least 4,200 stituches are taken each season in the hides of the 252 players who toil for the league's 14 teams.

Why so much gore in a game in which players are paid, at least theoretically, to score goals, not to cut each other up? Part of the answer is that violence is sanctioned, if not encouraged, by the NHL. "We've got to stamp out this sort of thing," said former Toronto Maple Leaf boss Conn Smythe, "or people are going to keep on buying tickets."

In fact, the rules of the game are arranged to encourage violence. A player is allowed to hit another with his body. It's called a body check. And he is permitted to use his stick to take the puck away from an opposing player. But the line between what is legal and what's not is so thin that few players have time to think about niceties. "You don't think," says Glen Sather, the rugged blond forward. "When you get hit, you hit back. *Then* you think."

Not only that, but there is an arsenal of potential weapons available at the drop of a puck: bulky elbow pads, knifelike skate blades, thick leather gauntlets with washboard backs, and a five-foot stick with a pointed tip. Put all these weapons to work in an 85-by-200 foot rink, surrounded by thick, inflexible three-and-a-half-foot-high wooden boards, and you have the makings of a cock pit.

There's another factor. NHL players learn early to live with pain. Boston center Derek Sanderson recalls getting his first lesson in hockey stoicism as an eight-year-old in Ontario. "During a practice session, a puck hit me right in the head, and the blood began to flow. Well, I had never seen blood like that before, and it made me sick. So I skated over to my father and shouted, 'I'm bleeding.' He gave me the once-over and snapped, 'You're all right, for Christ's sake. Get back out there. The blood will dry. Shake it off.' So I bled the entire practice, and when it was over, he took me to a hospital where I had three stitches. A few days later, the doctor pulled the stitches out, and my father kept them. When we got home, he put them in a little plastic box. He saved every one of my first 100 stitches. Soon I started to become proud of them. I'd come home after a tough game and say, 'Hi, Dad, eight more.' "

Glen Sather remembers seeing one of his teen-age teammates take a skate blade in his face. "The gash was so big you could see all of his teeth through it. It took 50 stitches to close it." The sewing took place between periods, and the lad didn't lose a minute of ice time. "Our coach made it clear this was the way to do things—to have the courage to come back and play after having your face slashed in half," Sather says. "I learned then you'd get praise from the coach if you were man enough to stay in the game after you were injured."

Despite all the blood and stoic energy expended, hockey players are easily the lowest paid big-league athletes.

"We're not paid enough for the abuse we take," Sather says. "But you don't think about this when you sign your contract. You only think about it after games, when you're patching up your wounds."

In 20 years of pro hockey, Larry Zeidel never gave injuries much thought, and he never made more than $15,000 a season. When he retired from the Philadelphia club three seasons ago, his face looked like a railroad map. He had fractured his skull twice. About 600 stitches had been taken in his hide. The only Jewish boy in a very tough Montreal neighborhood, he learned to be rough early in life. "You had to fight to survive," says Zeidel, who is now a stockbroker. "I had no choice, so I fought." Later on, he fought in the Quebec League, the Western League, the American League and the NHL.

While playing for the Edmonton Flyers of the Western League, Zeidel was involved in one battle so bloody and so intense it is still famous among hockey players, a group as blasé about blood as butchers. Jack Evans, lantern-jawed defenseman of the Saskatoon Quakers, provided the opposition. Zeidel doesn't remember how the fight started. "Evans hit me with his stick. I don't know if it was an accident or not, but it didn't matter. I had to get back at him. So I hit him with my stick."

The two of them went at it like medieval gladiators. First, they broke their sticks by banging them on each other's heads. Then they carved at each other with the jagged tumps. Covered with blood, they began to trade punches. Finally they wrestled each other to the ice, exhausted. "As we were being led from the ice," Zeidel remembers, "I noticed I was bleeding more than Evans. So I grabbed a loose stick and hit him over the head with it. Funny, but I remember holding back just a little bit as I hit him. If I hadn't restrained myself, he'd be dead."

Hockey fights are getting so rough that in the summer of 1970 Keith Magnuson of the Chicago Black Hawks took boxing lessons from bantamweight champion Johnny Coulon. In his first bout of the season, Magnuson went against Earl Heiskala of Philadelphia. Magnuson took him out with one punch. It could be a trend.

"When I see a fight coming," says Sanderson, "I actually feel the adrenalin pumping through me. For a second, I feel weak, then, suddenly, I'm strong. Once I start swinging, the only thing I worry about is my eyes. Sometimes a player will kick you in the face, so I try to protect my cheekbones and my eyes."

Sanderson, mustachioed and sideburned, is known for battling spectators as well as other players. In Philadelphia, (December 1970) he instigated a mass brawl involving players and fans. "Two guys started saying things about my mother," Sanderson said. "You can only take so much." Sanderson jumped the fans, and his teammates rallied to his assistance. "They were terrible," said one fan. "They used their skates to kick at people, and they called the cops 'pigs.' "

The Bruins seem to operate—successfully—on the theory that the team that slays together, plays together. Their mass-attack style was introduced during the regime of coach Harry Sinden, who would say to his team: "If you kids want to do something out there, if you want to fight or you want to hit, do it. You've got 18 of the world's toughest men on your side."

Brian Conacher, formerly of Toronto, was one of the first to learn that Sinden was serious. In a game against Boston, Conacher, finding himself on a collision course with the great Bobby Orr, lifted his stick to face level. Orr slammed into it and fell to the ice, blood spurting from his nose. "The next thing I knew," says Conacher, "Johnny McKenzie jumped on my back and then Orr piled on." Conacher was so viciously beaten that even the Boston *Globe* felt called upon to condemn the brutality.

Orr copped the routine hockey plea. "Conacher got me in the nose, and I was bleeding like a stuck pig. I didn't want to fight, but if they see you backing up in this league—well, they'll run you out."

The Bruins profit by this kind of thinking. Their style, which is fast becoming the new style of the '70's, is to hit, hit, hit; then, when the opposition has been softened up, score. "Hockey has changed for the worse," says Conacher, who quit the game in disgust in his prime, at age 27, to become a sports telecaster. "Players are not succeeding because they are good hockey players, but because they are good woodchoppers. It makes me sick, because they're taking the skills out of the game. Take Sanderson. He doesn't have to play that rough. But he's found he's more marketable going for blood."

Despite all the mayhem, only two major-league players have actually died as the result of hockey injuries. In 1907, Owen McCourt, the leading scorer of the then big-league Cornwall, Ontario, team, died after being hit on the head with a stick. In 1968, Bill Masterton of the Minnesota North Stars tripped trying to skate between two defenders, fell headfirst on the ice and cracked his skull on the hard, rutted surface. He died two days later, and once again a clamor arose to make protective helmets mandatory equipment.

Although far from perfect, the helmets do provide some measure of protection. No team has forbidden their use, but some coaches quietly convince players that they should not wear them. A few stars like Stan Mikita of Chicago and Phil Goyette of Buffalo wear helmets all the time. For the most part, though, players themselves refuse to. "They're too hot," says Sather. Probably more important, though, is that old Canadian *machismo*.

Dave Balon, who passed the puck to Masterton on that ill-fated play, put on a helmet after the accident. But he soon began to get little flyers from North Star manager Wren Blair. "He bugged me about wearing it," Balon says. When Balon was traded to New York in 1968, he began wearing a helmet again, along with teammates Larry Jeffrey and Phil Goyette. Soon, though, the Rangers traded both Jeffrey and Goyette. Balon got the message. He took the helmet off.

Balon's boss, Ranger manager—coach Emile "The Cat" Francis, insists anyone who wants to can wear a helmet. But he says all the time that hockey—like life—is a risky game. This may explain why he traded away helmet-wearer Red Berenson, now a star for the Detroit Red Wings, and proved that on some clubs, helmet wearing is one of the game's many risks.

Once the Bruin management tried to force its players to wear helmets. They refused. "Helmets turn me off," says

Sanderson. "If you wear one, it means you're conscious of injury, and if you are, you better get out of this game."

The reasoning may be flawed. Goaltenders have long taken up the face mask—once considered both sissified and hindering. Only two of the 28 NHL goalies—Gump Worsley of Minnesota and Joe Daley of Detroit—now play without masks. Not that masks always prevent goalies from being injured. "When a player like Bobby Hull shoots the puck," says Pittsburgh goalie Les Binkley, "it comes so fast it looks like a little pea. One of these days, that shot of Hull's will kill somebody."

Injuries to goalies are seldom deliberate. It is the flagrant woodchopping and rioting that at times inspire cries of barbarism in the Canadian Parliament. When that happens, there is usually a promise of a crackdown.

In December 1970 NHL President Clarence Campbell handed out an impressive-sounding $15,850 in fines to NHL players and clubs and said, "This type of senseless brawling has got to stop." But the fact is that nobody pays much attention to these fines. "If you can't beat 'em in an alley, you can't beat 'em on the ice," Conn Smythe told his Toronto players. The custom is for the club to pay any fines levied for fighting. So players respond with passion and flailing sticks.

Still, there is fear that one day a fatality will occur as the result of a fight, and then legislators will do what Campbell has not. Recently, a Quebec judge observed unhappily: "One gets the impression that hockey players believe there will be no police intervention and no criminal charges regardless of what they do on the ice."

When Vancouver's Wayne Maki sent Ted Green of Boston to the hospital with a fractured skull in 1969 (Green is believed to have started the fight), there were arrests, but no sentences. Both were acquitted on charges of assault. The only result was that Green, a plastic plate in his head, now wears an odd-looking helmet of his own design. And he's still fighting. Less than a month after he returned to action, he ripped off his helmet and went at it with Dan Maloney of the Chicago Black Hawks. "It's part of the game," Green said.

Which may explain why the Toronto *Telegram* once headlined a story, "IT'S NOT A GAME, IT'S A WAR!" And until more players are killed, it will remain just that.

THE BLACK HAWKS AND THEIR BLACK CLOUD

WHETHER it's apocryphal or not, a legend has spread through the National Hockey League that the Chicago Black Hawks forever will skate under the black cloud of a jinx that is now 45 years old.

No matter how good the Windy City sextet may be, they almost always appear doomed in the end—all because of the curse of Pete Muldoon. It certainly seemed to be the case last spring when the Canadiens whipped Chicago in the Cup finals.

In 1926 Muldoon coached the Hawks to a third-place finish, which was considered superb for their first year of big-league play. But the Black Hawks' eccentric owner, Major Frederic McLaughlin, thought his club should have finished first.

When Muldoon protested, McLaughlin fired him, never thinking that a hex was about to be cast over Chicago hockey. "Fire me, major," Muldoon supposedly said, "and you'll never finish first! I'll put a curse on this team that will hoodoo it 'till the end of time!"

The major laughed at first, but events dating right up to the present suggest that there was more to "The Muldoon Curse" than the Black Hawks bosses would care to admit. In their 45-year history the Black Hawks have finished first only three times. And, if Pete Muldoon suffered a slump in those years his curse took over again in the playoffs, as it did in May 1971 when Chicago was wiped out.

Muldoon curse or not, the Black Hawks have become the Dallas Cowboys of hockey, the team that couldn't win in the clutch. In the 1969-70 season, for example, they did finish on top of the NHL's East Divison as goalie Tony Esposito set a league record with 15 shutouts. The Boston Bruins weren't impressed.

"I didn't think Tony was that good," snapped Derek Sanderson. "And he was a little cocky. But we cooled him off. By the second game we discovered that the Hawks only had a couple of guys willing to mix it—Keith Magnuson and Cliff Koroll. The rest were just standing around in awe watching Bobby Orr fly."

Boston wiped out Chicago in four games. Coach Billy Reay's club did finish first in 1970-71, its first year in the West Division, because of four very interesting hockey players—Stan Mikita, Bobby Hull, Magnuson and Esposito.

Troubled by a bad back, the helmeted Mikita continually proves that there's room for a good little man in hockey. Despite his physical woes the 5-9, 165-pound center finished 17th in the scoring race last season but also excelled defensively. He vividly proved that one night in November while "killing" a penalty for his club against the Rangers at Chicago Stadium.

The puck skimmed to All-Star defenseman Brad Park of the Rangers at the blue line. Park wound up for a shot but Mikita threw himself in front of the puck, deflecting it harmlessly into the New York zone. He then duped Park into a penalty and the Black Hawks turned a 1-0 deficit into a 2-1 victory. "Mikita did it all by himself," said Rangers' general manager-coach Emile Francis. "He can beat you a lot of different ways."

In contrast with the workmanlike Mikita is Chicago's "Golden Jet," Bobby Hull. Once the NHL's number one draw, Hull has been deposed in that area by Bobby Orr of the Bruins. Hull, the Samson of hockey, is losing his hair; and everybody knows what happened to Samson when his locks disappeared. Hull has lost something of his old-time *élan* and his once-devastating shot appears a trifle more manageable by NHL goalies. But he still moves like a speeding bull and when provoked he'll gore anybody. He nearly decapitated Syl Apps of the Pittsburgh Penguins last season with a series of uppercuts after Apps had checked him illegally.

"I wouldn't want to have another fight with him," said Apps when it was over. "He's too strong for me."

Normally, coach Billy Reay would prefer that Hull concentrate on scoring and leave the socking to defenseman Keith Magnuson, the man who took boxing lessons. I learned a lot about footwork," said Magnuson who led the league last season with 291 penalty minutes. "Even though I'm on skates I find it helps."

As the Black Hawk policeman, Magnuson nurtured some incendiary grudges around the League. He clashed frequently with such hitters as New York's Vic Hadfield and Orland Kurtenbach of Vancouver the resident heavyweight champion of the NHL.

Once, Magnuson, floored husky Earl Heiskala with a six inch jab. "You don't see many like it," said a veteran defenseman. "Earl's knees buckled like a pillar in an earthquake."

Other tough guys around the league have come to appreciate Magnuson for his seemingly boundless energy. "He's aggressive, eager and he's got a lot of nervous strength," said Sanderson. "He's so awfully tight that he reacts quickly to situations. He doesn't quit and he's tough to beat."

When Magnuson and defense-mates fail there's always goalie Esposito to blunt the enemy assault. There are those who believe that Tony, the Montreal Canadiens' castoff, was the man responsible for lifting Chicago from last place in 1969 to the top in 1970, a feat never before was accomplished in the NHL.

Strangely enough, Esposito's style is virtually indescribable. He somehow manages to keep the puck out. "This guy is like Johnny Bower was when I was with Toronto," said teammate Jim Pappin. "He doesn't even want you to score on him in practice."

Esposito's competitiveness is so high he finds it impossible even to play golf for the fun of it. "I don't like to play any sport for relaxation," said Esposito. "I go out to win. The only way I can relax is to go to a movie."

Sharing the goaltending with Esposito is chunky Gerry Desjardins, regarded by some observers as the equal if not superior to Esposito. However, the thoughtful Desjardins has X-rayed Tony's style and insists that Esposito can do more than any goaltender in captivity.

"Tony has a way of dropping to his knees and spreading his pads out to either side on certain kinds of shots," Desjardins explained. "Mostly, they are shots from the point. That way he's in better shape to take care of rebounds than I am after I've done the splits on the same kind of shot.

"Another great thing he does is give the shooter a target between his pads; then he drops down at the last second to close it off. His timing is terrific and he always seems to know exactly where the puck is, even with his back turned."

While Desjardins is resigned to a spot in the shadow, another Black Hawk shares similar sentiments; Dennis Hull, the Golden Jet's kid brother. Dennis differs markedly from his older brother in style, ability and personality.

The younger Hull is less flamboyant than Bobby and lacks The Golden Jet's ease of skating. Coach Billy Reay has stressed checking more than scoring with Dennis, a fact that has not disturbed young Hull.

"When I got into this league," said Dennis, "I realized that if I scored 20 goals a season, I'd be doing all right." He managed to reach 30 three years ago when the Hawks finished last and he dipped to 17 in 1969-70 when they wound up on top, which says something about the value of checking. Last season he scored 40.

"Bobby has scored 50 or more goals in four separate years." said Dennis, "and I know that many people have wondered if I could do anything like that. If it bugged me not to be as good as Bobby, I never realized it.

"I know what I can do. I know I can't skate with him and I can't shoot with him. There's only one thing for me to do—play my position, do the simple things like watching my man and being sure he doesn't score. At no time have I ever felt any sort of jealousy for Bobby, just admiration."

Cracking the lineup of a first-place team with names like Hull, Hull, Mikita, Magnuson and Esposito was never more difficult than it was last season. This explains why left wing Dan Maloney is regarded as a cut above the average by the Chicago front office. Because the Black Hawks won The Prince of Wales Trophy in 1970 they were forced to scrape the bottom of the NHL draft barrel. They were fortunate to come up with the 6-1, 185-pound Maloney.

"All I wanted was a chance to play for the team that drafted me," he said. "When it was Chicago, I wondered if I'd get the chance. After all, they finished first the previous year."

Coach Billy Reay spotted Maloney on a line with Pit Martin and Gerry Pinder. He responded with two goals and three assists in his first six games of 1970-71. What's more, he set up the winning goals in each of Chicago's first three victories.

"In one game," recalled Reay, "he went into the corner and knocked down the opposing player who had possession of the puck. "One of our guys picked it up and we went on to score."

There are those who believe that Magnuson and Maloney epitomize the new Black Hawks, a club that must check hard to win. "The game I have to play is hitting," said Maloney. "If I'm aggressive I'll get points."

Several experts believe the accent on textbook, checking hockey should have brought the Black Hawks the Stanley Cup last Spring. Perhaps they forgot about the Muldoon jinx.

TABLE HOCKEY GOES BIG TIME

IT WAS four hours before the World Table Hockey Championships were to begin and my partner—who also happens to be my wife, Shirley,—turned fearfully to me and downed two aspirins.

"Are you *SURE* we did the right things?" she said, obviously doubting my game plan. "Just because Gordie

Howe once did it that doesn't mean it'll work for table hockey."

Instead of preparing a pre-game meal of steak and salad, I had insisted we have a chocolate milk shake. Howe once told me he did that and then scored a couple of goals that night when he was a rookie up from Omaha. "What's good enough for Gordie Howe," I told her, "is good enough for me!"

Who could blame her for having butterflies? After years of playing in the minor leagues of table hockey, we now were up against the best players ever to grace the parlors from Montreal to Manhattan. A mile away, in a cavernous apartment on New York's West Side overlooking the Hudson River, "Mister Hockey" (he even copyrighted the name) Pierre Delfausse of Montreal, supervised workmen who were putting the final touches on the two championship tables. It was Delfausse, the Lord Stanley of Preston of table hockey, who introduced the sliding players to the sport and thus led us to the modern, firewagon style.

Although Delfausse helped design the modern game, tourney play itself was developed under the aegis of Ira Gitler, a New York jazz writer; Michael Hopp, a young plastics industrialist; and Richard Selby, a millinery buyer who's been keeping a bottle of champagne in his refrigerator 31 years, awaiting the day when the Rangers win the Stanley Cup.

"While we were waiting," said Gitler, "we thought we owed it to ourselves to enjoy the thrill of a hockey championship. Who knows, the Rangers may not win the Cup for another 30 years."

So, Gitler and friends started a table hockey championship on an informal basis eight years ago, and it immediately caught on. One night, Camille Henry, then a Ranger left wing, attended a tournament; he masqueraded under the name of Wally Whipachowsky to avoid punishment from the management. Each year there were more and more players until three years ago when a trophy was offered to the winning team. It happened to be my wife's silver gravy bowl which was rechristened The Harold Cup for the occasion.

For two years the team of Gitler and Robert Blume, a

page at the National Broadcasting Company, annexed the Cup. However, mounting criticism of the tourney's shabbiness and my wife's desire to take the Harold Cup out of play and return it to the kitchen, brought about a revolution in big-league table hockey.

A meeting of the Board of Governors was held and despite protests from established cities that it would result in a dilution of talent the czars voted to expand into Canada and offer a cash prize ($40) to the winning team. Now that table hockey had gone professional, a new trophy was struck and the game was officially big-league.

"I'm worried about those ringers from Montreal," said Shirley as our cab deposited us in front of the tourney entrance where a crowd had already gathered. "I hear they practice this game with *real* ice."

Sure enough, players had begun filtering in for some tune-up matches while referee-in-chief Richard Friedman in his black-and-white striped shirt checked the underside of each game. He remembered that the 1968 series had been marred by charges of sabotage when the Breu-Hopp team simultaneously broke two springs during a three-man scoring attack late in a game. "Plier-marks on the spring edges convinced me of foul-play," said Hopp, the foremost exponent of table hockey's jam-shot.

My wife's fears were well-founded. Thinking we had obtained a psychological edge by wearing our traditional New York Ranger jerseys, we were stunned to the core when the team of Christopher and Jonathan Cerf entered in the official regalia of the Pittsburgh Penguins. "I told you expansion would ruin the game," she insisted, "These fellows look like a bunch of woodchoppers."

Woodchoppers or not, I immediately realized that the Cerfs were not to be treated lightly. Of the 26 competing teams they were placed—at 9-1 odds—seventh in the official seeding list distributed at the press arena adjacent to the bar. At the top, of course, was the Gitler-Blume combine with this description: "Original winners of the Harold Cup, emblematic of amateur table hockey supremacy. Holders of the Pagello Trophy for goaltending and inventors of the off-the-board stall ploy (since declared illegal). They are rated even-money favorites."

Tops among the Canadian entries was Montreal television actor Dino Narizzano ("Search for Tomorrow") and his artist-wife, Aleen, whose father was a champion rugby player in England, and herself was a superb field hockey player. "I am hoping," said Aleen, "that there is a carry-over from field to table hockey."

Seasoned observers agreed that the Canadians would have difficulty capturing the shiny gold T. J. Rugg Trophy, emblem of world table hockey supremacy. The Rugg commemorates the nervous breakdown suffered by the Detroit team of Rugg and Rugg during the 1969 semi-finals following a Mickey Hopp jam-shot in the ribs.

Already the metallic clinking of the players could be heard in the background as warm-up matches got underway. Sal Marchiano, a New York sportscaster and Sheldon Sakowtiz of the Associated Press moved over to rinkside where the Gitler-Blume team was tuning up. "Tenacity and utter concentration are the keys to the championship," said Gitler. "Tilting the board doesn't hurt either."

"Wait a minute," I protested, "isn't there an official rulebook for the professional game?"

With the split-second speed of a John Ashley, referee-in-chief Friedman produced the rules of play. Sure enough, tilting was illegal under punishment of a penalty shot. In addition, the rulebook stated: "A penalty shot shall also be called for unsportsmanlike deportment, too many men on the ice, insulting the referee, and physically assaulting your opponents (or your teammate)."

Friedman also pointed out that all preliminary games would be of five-minute duration and, in case of tie, sudden-death overtime would decide the match. The quarter and semi-finals would consist of three five-minute periods and the final would be a best-of-three game affair. Shortly before game time, a crisis erupted. For the first time in table hockey history an all-female team had challenged for the Cup, and, in turn, was being challenged by several male entrants. The Board of Governors held a hurried star chamber meeting, closed to the press. However, a listener overheard them gleefully approve the application with the comment, "Their expected defeat will strike a blow for men's liberation." And so the team of Jane Burton and Cheryl Weed was pitted against Sandy Burton and Peter Weed.

In the opening rounds there would be two games operating in two different rooms until the quarter-finals when all matches would be played on the grandstand center court. It had been hoped to have National Hockey League President Clarence Campbell on hand for the opening face-off, but rumor had it that he was away attending a riot.

The selection committee announced our opening-round foes would be the Cerf Brothers. "That's not fair," my wife complained, "they've come with their own cheering section," Sure enough, Jonathan was accompanied by a lovely lady armed with a Pittsburgh Penguin banner and an unusually high decibel count.

I turned to referee-in-chief Friedman with a word of caution. "Keep your eye on the woman," I said. "People have warned me that if we get a breakaway, she's instructed to throw chopped liver on the ice to disrupt our forwards." The referee was not impressed.

Suddenly, a hush fell over the room; the houselights dimmed; and from a hi-fi set came the strains of the *Star Spangled Banner* followed by *O Canada*. "I'm touched," said Robert Stampleman, another Montrealer entered in the tourney, who appeared visibly moved. "I'm going out to win this one for The Rocket." Only later it was learned that he was referring to Rocket Robillard, his bookie.

Now it was game time. I gulped down a sedative and assured my wife that it was not unusual to be nauseaous before the opening face-off. "Then why aren't *they* upset?" she demanded.

It was true. Our opponents, the Cerf Brothers, seemed as calm and assured as the Boston Bruins playing a peewee team from Kapuskasing, Ontario.

Our strategy was simple enough. I manned the three metal rods on the left side of the table; which moved the left wing, left defense and goaltender. Shirley handled the other three, center, right wing and right defense. We decided to use the game plan which had worked so well in the Harold Cup matches during our junior table hockey days: both the left and right wings would feed passes to our center, hoping for a direct shot on goal. But, already, the Cerfs were beginning the psychological warfare which ultimately would destroy us.

"I hear she doesn't backcheck," Christopher whispered to Jonathan, just loud enough so that we could hear them.

"That's right," Jonathan acknowledged. "And they tell me he's afraid to mix it in the corners; a real snow-thrower."

Backchecking. Snowthrowing. Surely they couldn't be serious. But, then again, maybe they were, and I began worrying. Before I knew it the referee had dropped the puck and the rinkside crowd was roaring. We were now in the midst of table hockey's Stanley Cup.

"Skate, *skate*," I shouted at my wife, losing all control of my mental processes. "Sorry dear, I mean, push, *push*."

The Cerfs quietly launched their attack, controlling the puck as if it was magnetized. "They are playing textbook table hockey," murmured an admiring rinksider as Christopher skimmed a pass to Jonathan in the center. His shot was into the net before I could swing my goaltender to the left. "It's those damned curved sticks," I muttered and prepared to resume play.

Within two minutes the Cerfs had built up a 4-0 lead and it appeared only a protest or irregularity of some kind would save us. I considered reaching under the table and snapping all the springs on their forwards but Shirley said that might appear obvious. Besides, it wouldn't be right to threaten the tournament with scandal.

Apart from the crusade for female participation the table hockey tournament had been shaken by only one major scandal. Two years ago Garrison Frant of Detroit was caught attempting to substitute his own game for the official championship model. Frant's version was an exact replica of the original except that the Detroit challenger had carefully filed down the sides of the centerman's opening. On cross-examination later, Frant explained his ploy: "I calculated that by natural friction of ten minutes of heated play in the finals the center opening would be widening by a fraction of an inch, but just enough to allow the centerman to fall through the aperture. Since rules state that in the event of injury, play continues until the next face-off I figured I could score at least one goal and thereby win the game." The action, of course, disqualified Frant from winning the Lady Remoser of Winfield Trophy for good sportsmanship.

To avoid a repetition of a similar scandal, each game is moved directly from Pierre Delfausse's factory to a safe deposit vault where it remains until two hours before tournament time. This promptly produced complaints of chippy ice and bouncy pucks, a defect which was eliminated last year by keeping the black discs refrigerated until the start of play.

The Cerfs maintained their bombardment through our game and led, 5-0 with one minute remaining. "Let's pull our goalie," I urged my wife, "and play with six skaters. At least we might break the shutout."

By this time, however, she wasn't even talking to me. And, as the siren wailed ending the game she stalked away in a snit, closely followed by reporters. "Punch Imlach was right," she told interviewers. "There's no way a man can play winning hockey wearing a beard. NO WAY!" Before reporters could get to me I slammed the door to the foyer, which happened to be the dressing room, and snapped that I would not talk to them.

After a four-minute pout I finally allowed the reporters in for a chat. I allowed that the Cerfs had shown me nuances I had never dreamed possible. They had truly brought stick-handling and pattern passing back to the game. The newsmen were not impressed. "Obviously, you haven't seen some of the other East Division teams," said one of them. "The Hopp-Breu combine looks like a real threat and so do the professional champions of Long Island."

I quickly consulted my program. The Long Island team consisted of Stan Isaacs, sports columnist for Newsday, and Marvin Kitman, author of "George Washington's Bank Account." They were seeded eighth with the following description: "Referee-baiters extraordinaire, this team holds the world's record for bench-penalties. Weak defensively, they could be trouble if Isaacs' infamous 'Hidden-defenseman—slap-shot' is working."

As things turned out, however, the Long Island champs were wiped out in an early round without so much as gaining a misconduct penalty. The Breu-Hopp team slashed their way to the finals against the redoubtable Cerfs, who had defeated the defending champs—Ira Gitler and Robert Blume—1-0 in sudden-death overtime on a disputed goal which rapidly bounced in and out of the cage.

It was now 1 A.M. and an air of controversy hung over the finals. Midway in the tournament it was discovered that Breu was wearing a plaster cast over his right arm. Veteran hockey observers remarked that it was a case of gutsiness rivalled only by Dickie Moore of the Montreal Canadiens who once won the NHL scoring championship while playing with a cast on his arm. However, skeptics charged that the cast was nothing but an illegal ploy.

"The cast definitely gives him an advantage," said Michael Widener, whose team was defeated in the semifinals. "It's too much weight to contend with. Besides, it gives him a psychological advantage. We didn't want to beat a man with a broken arm."

Hearing that, Hopp nearly came to blows with Widener. The linesmen finally separated the two and Hopp explained how Breu's cast actually was a detriment to their team. "It got in my way," Hopp insisted. "We would have done better without the cast. Personally, I'd prefer a cast of thousands."

"One more crack like that," snapped referee Friedman, "and I'll slap you with a misconduct."

Meanwhile, attendants surrounded the rink, checking all the equipment. Two workmen cleaned the playing surface with a chamois while the public address announcer called off the final lucky numbers for the grand prize of a 1971 set of Lincoln Logs. The stage was set for the table hockey final. Breu and Hopp each downed a glass of mineral water while the Cerf Brothers conferred with their chief scout, Jim Benagh, who had been spying on the Breu-Hopp team throughout the night.

"They're like the Bruins," said Benagh. "They'll try to intimidate you in the early minutes. But once they learn they can't run you out of the rink they'll choke," Benagh gave his men a crisp pat on the *derriére* and returned to his seat. "Hang tough, men!"

The public address announcer interrupted. "Attention," the man said. "There will be a prize of $40 for the winners." A wag from the sidelines interrupted. "Yeah, marked down from $42.50." The announcer continued. "In addition, the runners-up will win one table hockey game." Again, an interrupting. "Throw the game. Throw the game!"

Their eyes flashing fiercely, the opponents disregarded the barbs from the stands and lined up for the opening face-off. As expected, the Hopp-Breu team charged bullishly at the smaller Cerf Brothers while the smaller men dipsy-doodled around their bigger foes like Max and Doug Bentley of yesteryear.

"I can't get mad at those little guys," Hopp complained to his teammate. "If only they'd do something nasty."

With one-minute remaining in the first period, Christopher Cerf's center flung a backhander past Breu, giving them a 1-0 lead. They added another goal in the second period, forcing Breu and Hopp to open up. Meanwhile, Jonathan Cerf, the goaltender on the team, dancing and dodging, blocked the best shots his foes had to offer. Only later did he reveal that he had revolutionized the game with a new technique.

"I cover four men, leaving Chris with only two to handle," said Jonathan. "In this way I handle the goalie with my left hand and the other three with my right."

"He's a bulldog of a Penguin," said Benagh.

Sure enough, the Cerfs had broken the traditional style in which each player covered three rods and only too late did Hopp and Breu discover this. The Cerfs pumped home a third goal in the last period and won the opening game of the best-of-three final, 3-0.

"It was the penultimate in table hockey," said Gitler, "Or should I say Penguinultimate?"

"No, no," said Benagh, "it's quite a feather in the Penguins' cap, if I may mix a metaphor. A black and white feather at that."

Now it was time for the second game of the finals. The Cerfs had returned to their face-off position and so had

Hopp. But where was Breu? "I think he had a heart attack," said Hopp. Referee-in-chief Friedman pulled out his watch; he would give Breu two minutes to return to the rink or the championship would be forfeited. Suddenly, a messenger arrived with a communique: "HAD TO LEAVE. STOP. OUR BABY-SITTER THREATENED TO QUIT IF WE DIDN'T GET HOME. STOP. SEE YOU NEXT YEAR. BREU."

I turned to my wife. "Y'know," I said, "it's a good thing they don't play these games at Maple Leaf Gardens!"

P.S. The World Professional Table Hockey Championships *are* played every December in New York City.

BERENSON, GORDON ARTHUR (RED)
Born, Regina, Sask., December 8, 1939.
Center. Shoots left. 6', 190 lbs.
Last amateur club: University of Michigan.

Season	Club	Lea	Regular Schedule					Playoffs				
			GP	G	A	TP	PIM	GP	G	A	TP	PIM
1961-62	Mtl. Canadiens	NHL	4	1	2	3	4	5	2	0	2	0
1962-63	Hull-Ottawa	EPHL	30	23	25	48	28	—	—	—	—	—
1962-63	Mtl. Canadiens	NHL	37	2	6	8	15	5	0	0	0	0
1963-64	Mtl. Canadiens	NHL	69	7	9	16	12	7	0	0	0	4
1964-65	Quebec	AHL	65	22	34	56	16	5	1	2	3	8
1964-65	Mtl. Canadiens	NHL	3	1	2	3	0	9	0	1	1	2
1965-66	Quebec	AHL	34	17	36	53	14	6	1	5	6	2
1965-66	Mtl. Canadiens	NHL	23	3	4	7	12	—	—	—	—	—
1966-67	NY Rangers	NHL	30	0	5	5	2	4	0	1	1	2
1967-68	NY Rangers	NHL	19	2	1	3	2	—	—	—	—	—
	St. Louis	NHL	55	22	29	51	22	18	5	2	7	9
1968-69	St. Louis	NHL	76	35	47	82	43	12	7	3	10	20
1969-70	St. Louis	NHL	67	33	39	72	38	16	7	5	12	8
1970-71	St. Louis-Detroit	NHL	69	21	38	59	16					
	NHL Totals		452	127	182	309	166	76	21	12	33	45

Traded by Montreal to New York for Ted Taylor and Garry Peters, June 13, 1966. Traded by New York with Barclay Plager to St. Louis for Ron Stewart and Ron Attwell, November 29, 1967. Traded by St. Louis with Tim Ecclestone to Detroit for Garry Unger and Wayne Connolly, February, 1971.

COURNOYER, YVAN SERGE
Born, Drummondville, Que., November 22, 1943.
Right wing. Shoots left. 5'7", 165 lbs.
Last amateur club: Canadiens (Jrs.).

Season	Club	Lea	Regular Schedule					Playoffs				
			GP	G	A	TP	PIM	GP	G	A	TP	PIM
1963-64	Mtl. Canadiens	NHL	5	4	0	4	0	—	—	—	—	—
1964-65	Quebec	AHL	7	2	1	3	0	—	—	—	—	—
1964-65	Mtl. Canadiens	NHL	55	7	10	17	10	12	3	1	4	0
1965-66	Mtl. Canadiens	NHL	65	18	11	29	8	10	2	3	5	2
1966-67	Mtl. Canadiens	NHL	69	25	15	40	14	10	2	3	5	6
1967-68	Mtl. Canadiens	NHL	64	28	32	60	23	13	6	8	14	4
1968-69	Mtl. Canadiens	NHL	76	43	44	87	31	14	4	7	11	5
1969-70	Mtl. Canadiens	NHL	72	27	36	63	23					
1970-71	Mtl. Canadiens	NHL	65	37	36	73	21	20	10	12	22	6
	NHL Totals		471	189	184	373	130	78	27	34	51	23

DRYDEN, KENNETH
Born, Hamilton, Ont., August 7, 1947
Goaltender. Shoots left. 6'3½", 210 lbs.
Last amateur club: Canadian National Team.

Season	Club	Lea	Regular Schedule				Playoffs			
			GP	GA	SO	GAPG	GP	GA	SO	GAPG
1970-71	Mtl. Canadiens	NHL	6	9	0	1.65	20	61	0	3.00

a Won Conn Smythe Trophy.

ESPOSITO, PHILIP ANTHONY (PHIL)
Born, Sault Ste. Marie, Ont., February 20, 1942.
Center. Shoots left. 6'1", 195 lbs.
Last amateur club: St. Catharines (Jrs.).

Season	Club	Lea	Regular Schedule					Playoffs				
			GP	G	A	TP	PIM	GP	G	A	TP	PIM
1961-62	Sault Ste. Marie	EPHL	6	0	3	3	2	—	—	—	—	—
1962-63	St. Louis	EPHL	71	36	54	90	51	—	—	—	—	—
1963-64	St. Louis	CPHL	43	26	54	80	65	—	—	—	—	—
1963-64	Chicago	NHL	27	3	2	5	2	4	0	0	0	0
1964-65	Chicago	NHL	70	23	32	55	44	13	3	3	6	15
1965-66	Chicago	NHL	69	27	26	53	49	6	1	1	2	2
1966-67	Chicago	NHL	69	21	40	61	40	6	0	0	0	7
1967-68	Boston	NHL	74	35	*49	84	21	4	0	3	3	0
1968-69 abc	Boston	NHL	74	49	*77	*126	79	10	*8	*10	*18	8
1969-70	Boston	NHL	76	*43	56	99	50	14	*13	*14	*27	16
1970-71 ac	Boston	NHL	78	*76	76	*152	71	7	3	7	10	
	NHL Totals		537	277	358	635	358	64	28	38	66	48

a Won Art Ross Trophy.
b Won Hart Trophy.
c NHL record for points in regular season.
Traded to Boston by Chicago with Ken Hodge and Fred Stanfield for Gilles
Marotte, Pit Martin and Jack Norris, May 15, 1967.

FAVELL, DOUGLAS ROBERT (Doug)
Born, St. Catharines, Ont., April 5, 1945.
Goaltender. Shoots left. 5'10", 172 lbs.
Last amateur club: Niagara Falls (Jrs.).

Season	Club	Lea.	Regular Schedule				Playoffs			
			GP	GA	SO	GAPG	GP	GA	SO	GAPG
1965-66	Oklahoma City	CPHL	17⅔	59	0	3.33	—	—	—	—
1965-66	San Francisco	WHL	2	6	0	3.00	1⅔	10	0	6.00
1966-67	Oklahoma City	CPHL	31	88	1	2.83	—	—	—	—
1967-68	Philadelphia	NHL	36½	83	4	2.27	2	8	0	4.00
1968-69	Quebec	AHL	3⅓	16	0	4.82	—	—	—	—
1968-69	Philadelphia	NHL	20	71	1	3.56	1	5	0	5.00
1969-70	Philadelphia	NHL	13⅔	43	1	3.15	—	—	—	—
1970-71	Philadelphia	NHL	44	108	2	2.66	2	8	0	4.00
	NHL Totals		114⅙	305	8	2.68	5	21	0	4.20

Drafted by Philadelphia from Boston in expansion draft, June 6, 1967.

GIACOMIN, EDWARD
Born, Sudbury, Ont., June 6, 1939.
Goaltender. Shoots left. 5'11", 175 lbs.
Last amateur club: New York Rovers (EHL).

Season	Club	Lea	Regular Schedule				Playoffs			
			GP	GA	SO	GAPG	GP	GA	SO	GAPG
1959-60	Providence	AHL	1	4	0	4.00	—	—	—	—
1960-61	Providence	AHL	43	183	0	4.26	—	—	—	—
1961-62	Providence	AHL	40	144	2	3.60	—	—	—	—
1962-63	Providence	AHL	39	102	4	2.62	6	31	0	5.17
1963-64 a	Providence	AHL	69	232	*6	3.37	3	12	0	4.00
1964-65	Providence	AHL	59	226	0	3.84	—	—	—	—
1965-66	NY Rangers	NHL	35	128	0	3.66	—	—	—	—
1965-66	Baltimore	AHL	7	21	0	3.00	—	—	—	—
1966-67	NY Rangers	NHL	66⅓	173	*9	2.61	4	14	0	3.50
1967-68	NY Rangers	NHL	65⅔	160	*8	2.44	6	18	0	3.00
1968-69	NY Rangers	NHL	68½	175	7	2.55	3	10	0	3.33
1969-70 a	NY Rangers	NHL	69	163	6	2.36	4⅔	19	0	4.13
1970-71 b	NY Rangers	NHL	45	95	*8	2.15	12	28	0	2.21
		NHL Totals	349½	894	38	2.56	29⅔	89	0	2.97

HOWE, GORDON
Born, Floral, Sask., March 31, 1928.
Right wing. Shoots right. 6', 205 lbs.
Last amateur club: Saskatoon Lions Club Juveniles.

Season	Club	Lea	Regular Schedule					Playoffs				
			GP	G	A	TP	PIM	GP	G	A	TP	PIM
1945-46	Omaha	USHL	51	22	26	48	53	6	2	1	3	15
1946-47	Detroit	NHL	58	7	15	22	52	5	0	0	0	18
1947-48	Detroit	NHL	60	16	28	44	63	10	1	1	2	11
1948-49	Detroit	NHL	40	12	25	37	57	11	*8	3	*11	19
1949-50	Detroit	NHL	70	35	33	68	69	1	0	0	0	7
1950-51a	Detroit	NHL	70	*43	*43	*86	74	6	4	3	7	4
1951-52ab	Detroit	NHL	70	*47	39	*86	78	8	2	*5	*7	2
1952-53ab	Detroit	NHL	70	*49	*46	*95	57	6	2	5	7	2
1953-54a	Detroit	NHL	70	33	*48	*81	109	12	4	5	9	*31
1954-55	Detroit	NHL	64	29	33	62	68	11	*9	11	*20	24
1955-56	Detroit	NHL	70	38	41	79	100	10	3	9	12	8
1956-57ab	Detroit	NHL	70	*44	45	*89	72	5	2	5	7	6
1957-58b	Detroit	NHL	64	33	44	77	40	4	1	1	2	0
1958-59	Detroit	NHL	70	32	46	78	57	—	—	—	—	—
1959-60b	Detroit	NHL	70	28	45	73	46	6	1	5	6	4
1960-61	Detroit	NHL	64	23	49	72	30	11	4	11	*15	10
1961-62	Detroit	NHL	70	33	44	77	54	—	—	—	—	—
1962-63ab	Detroit	NHL	70	*38	48	*86	100	11	7	9	*16	22
1963-64	Detroit	NHL	69	26	47	73	70	14	*9	10	*19	16
1964-65	Detroit	NHL	70	29	47	76	104	7	4	2	6	20
1965-66	Detroit	NHL	70	29	46	75	83	12	4	6	10	12
1966-67	Detroit	NHL	69	25	40	65	53	—	—	—	—	—
1967-68	Detroit	NHL	74	39	43	82	53	—	—	—	—	—
1968-69	Detroit	NHL	76	44	59	103	58	—	—	—	—	—
1969-70	Detroit	NHL	76	31	40	71	58	4	2	0	2	2
1970-71	Detroit	NHL	63	23	29	52	38	—	—	—	—	—
		NHL Totals	1687	786	1023	1809	1643	154	67	91	158	218

a Art Ross Trophy.
b Hart Trophy.

HULL, ROBERT MARVIN (BOBBY)
Born, Point Anne, Ont., January 3, 1939.
Left wing. Shoots left. 5'10", 193 lbs.
Last amateur club: St. Catharines (Jrs.).

Season	Club	Lea	Regular Schedule					Playoffs				
			GP	G	A	TP	PIM	GP	G	A	TP	PIM
1957-58	Chicago	NHL	70	13	34	47	62	—	—	—	—	—
1958-59	Chicago	NHL	70	18	32	50	50	6	1	1	2	2
1959-60a	Chicago	NHL	70	*39	42	*81	68	3	1	0	1	2
1960-61	Chicago	NHL	67	31	25	56	43	12	4	10	14	4
1961-62a	Chicago	NHL	70	*50	34	*84	35	12	*8	5	13	10
1962-63	Chicago	NHL	65	31	31	62	27	5	*8	2	10	4
1963-64	Chicago	NHL	70	*43	44	87	50	7	2	5	7	2
1964-65cd	Chicago	NHL	61	39	32	71	32	14	*10	7	*17	27
1965-66ad	Chicago	NHL	65	*54	43	*97	70	6	2	2	4	10
1966-67	Chicago	NHL	66	*52	28	80	52	6	4	2	6	0
1967-68	Chicago	NHL	71	*44	31	75	39	11	4	6	10	15
1968-69b	Chicago	NHL	74	*58	49	107	48	—	—	—	—	—
1969-70	Chicago	NHL	61	38	29	67	8	8	3	8	11	2
1970-71	Chicago	NHL	78	44	52	96	32	18	11	14	25	16
		NHL Totals	**958**	**554**	**506**	**1060**	**616**	**108**	**58**	**62**	**120**	**94**

a Won Art Ross Trophy.
b NHL record for goals scored in regular season.
c Won Lady Byng Memorial Trophy.
d Won Hart Trophy.

KEON, DAVID MICHAEL (DAVE)
Born, Noranda, Que., March 22, 1940.
Center. Shoots left. 5'9", 163 lbs.
Last amateur club: St. Michael's College (Jrs.).

Season	Club	Lea	Regular Schedule					Playoffs				
			GP	G	A	TP	PIM	GP	G	A	TP	PIM
1959-60	Sudbury	EPHL	—	—	—	—	—	4	2	2	4	2
1960-61a	Toronto	NHL	70	20	25	45	6	5	1	1	2	0
1961-62b	Toronto	NHL	64	26	35	61	2	12	5	3	8	0
1962-63b	Toronto	NHL	68	28	28	56	2	10	7	5	12	0
1963-64	Toronto	NHL	70	23	37	60	6	14	7	2	9	2
1964-65	Toronto	NHL	65	21	29	50	10	6	2	2	4	2
1965-66	Toronto	NHL	69	24	30	54	4	4	0	2	2	0
1966-67c	Toronto	NHL	66	19	33	52	2	12	3	5	8	0
1967-68	Toronto	NHL	67	11	37	48	4	—	—	—	—	—
1968-69	Toronto	NHL	75	27	34	61	12	4	1	3	4	2
1969-70	Toronto	NHL	72	32	30	62	6	—	—	—	—	—
1970-71	Toronto	NHL	76	38	38	76	4	6	3	2	5	0
		NHL Totals	**762**	**269**	**356**	**625**	**58**	**73**	**29**	**25**	**54**	**6**

a Won Calder Memorial Trophy.
b Won Lady Byng Memorial Trophy.
c Won Conn Smythe Trophy.

MAHOVLICH, FRANCIS WILLIAM (FRANK)
Born, Timmins, Ont., January 10, 1938.
Left wing. Shoots left. 6', 205 lbs.
Last amateur club: St. Michael's College (Jrs.).

			Regular Schedule					Playoffs				
Season	Club	Lea	GP	G	A	TP	PIM	GP	G	A	TP	PIM
1956-57	Toronto	NHL	3	1	0	1	2	—	—	—	—	—
1957-58a	Toronto	NHL	67	20	16	36	67	—	—	—	—	—
1958-59	Toronto	NHL	63	22	27	49	94	12	6	5	11	18
1959-60	Toronto	NHL	70	18	21	39	61	10	3	1	4	27
1960-61	Toronto	NHL	70	48	36	84	131	5	1	1	2	6
1961-62	Toronto	NHL	70	33	38	71	87	12	6	6	12	*29
1962-63	Toronto	NHL	67	36	37	73	56	9	0	2	2	8
1963-64	Toronto	NHL	70	26	29	55	66	14	4	*11	15	20
1964-65	Toronto	NHL	59	23	28	51	76	6	0	3	3	9
1965-66	Toronto	NHL	68	32	24	56	68	4	1	0	1	10
1966-67	Toronto	NHL	63	18	28	46	44	12	3	7	10	8
1967-68	Toronto	NHL	50	19	17	36	30	—	—	—	—	—
	Detroit	NHL	13	7	9	16	2	—	—	—	—	—
1968-69	Detroit	NHL	76	49	29	78	38	—	—	—	—	—
1969-70	Detroit	NHL	74	38	32	70	59	4	0	0	0	2
1970-71	Detroit-Montreal	NHL	73	31	42	73	41	20	14	13	27	18
	NHL Totals		956	421	413	834	922	108	38	49	87	155

a Won Calder Memorial Trophy.
Traded to Detroit by Toronto with Garry Unger, Pete Stemkowski and rights to Carl Brewer for Paul Henderson, Norm Ullman and Floyd Smith, March 3, 1968. Traded to Montreal for Mickey Redmond, Bill Collins and Guy Cherron in February 1971.

ORR, ROBERT GORDON (BOBBY)
Born, Parry Sound, Ont., March 20, 1948.
Defense. Shoots left. 5'11", 180 lbs.
Last amateur club: Oshawa, Ont. (Jrs.).

			Regular Schedule					Playoffs				
Season	Club	Lea	GP	G	A	TP	PIM	GP	G	A	TP	PIM
1966-67a	Boston	NHL	61	13	28	41	102	—	—	—	—	—
1967-68b	Boston	NHL	46	11	20	31	63	4	0	2	2	2
1968-69b	Boston	NHL	67	21	43	64	133	10	1	7	8	10
1969-70 bcdefg	Boston	NHL	76	33	*87	*120	125	14	9	11	20	14
1970-71 fb	Boston	NHL	78	37	*102	139	91	7	4	8	12	10
	NHL Totals		328	115	280	395	514	35	14	28	42	36

a Won Calder Memorial Trophy.
b Won James Norris Memorial Trophy.
c NHL record for goals in regular season by a defenseman.
d NHL record for assists in regular season.
e Won Art Ross Trophy.
f Won Hart Trophy.
g Won Conn Smythe Trophy.

PARK, DOUGLAS BRADFORD (BRAD)
Born, Toronto, Ont., July 6, 1948.
Defense. Shoots left. 6', 190 lbs.
Last amateur club: Toronto Marlboros (Jrs.).

Season	Club	Lea	Regular Schedule					Playoffs				
			GP	G	A	TP	PIM	GP	G	A	TP	PIM
1968-69	Buffalo	AHL	17	2	12	14	49	—	—	—	—	—
1968-69	NY Rangers	NHL	54	3	23	26	70	4	0	2	2	7
1969-70	NY Rangers	NHL	60	11	26	37	98	5	1	2	3	11
1970-71	NY Rangers	NHL	68	7	37	44	114	13	0	3	3	42
		NHL Totals	182	21	86	107	282	22	1	7	8	60

PERREAULT, GILBERT (Gil)
Born, Victoriaville, Que., Nov. 13, 1950.
Center. Shoots left. 5' 11½", 183 lbs.
Last amateur club: Montreal Jr. Canadiens (OHA).

Season	Club	Lea	Regular Schedule					Playoffs				
			GP	G	A	TP	PIM	GP	A	A	TP	PIM
1970-71a	Buffalo	NHL	78	38	34	72	19	—	—	—	—	—
		NHL Totals	78	38	34	72	19					

a Won Calder Memorial Trophy.

SANDERSON, DEREK MICHAEL
Born, Niagara Falls, Ont., June 16, 1946.
Center. Shoots left. 6', 176 lbs.
Last amateur club: Niagara Falls Flyers (Jrs.).

Season	Club	Lea	Regular Schedule					Playoffs				
			GP	G	A	TP	PIM	GP	G	A	TP	PIM
1965-66	Oklahoma City	CPHL	2	1	0	1	0	4	0	4	4	5
1965-66	Boston	NHL	2	0	0	0	0	—	—	—	—	—
1966-67	Boston	NHL	2	0	0	0	0	—	—	—	—	—
1966-67	Oklahoma City	CPHL	—	—	—	—	—	2	0	0	0	0
1967-68a	Boston	NHL	71	24	25	49	98	4	0	2	2	9
1968-69	Boston	NHL	61	26	22	48	146	9	*8	2	10	36
1969-70	Boston	NHL	50	18	23	41	118	14	5	4	9	72
1970-71	Boston	NHL	71	29	34	63	130	7	2	1	3	13
	NHL Totals		257	97	104	201	492	34	15	9	24	130

a Won Calder Memorial Trophy.

UNGER, GARRY DOUGLAS
Born, Edmonton, Alta., December 7, 1947.
Center. Shoots left. 5'11", 170 lbs.
Last amateur club: London Nationals (Jrs.).

Season	Club	Lea	Regular Schedule					Playoffs				
			GP	G	A	TP	PIM	GP	G	A	TP	PIM
1966-67	Tulsa	CPHL	2	2	0	2	2	—	—	—	—	—
1966-67	Rochester	AHL	1	0	0	0	0	1	0	0	0	0
1967-68	Rochester	AHL	5	1	3	4	6	—	—	—	—	—
1967-68	Tulsa	CPHL	9	3	5	8	6	—	—	—	—	—
1967-68	Toronto	NHL	15	1	1	2	4	—	—	—	—	—
	Detroit	NHL	13	5	10	15	2	—	—	—	—	—
1968-69	Detroit	NHL	76	24	20	44	33	—	—	—	—	—
1969-70	Detroit	NHL	76	42	24	66	67	4	0	1	1	6
1970-71	Detroit-St. Louis	NHL	79	28	28	56	104	6	3	2	5	—
	NHL Totals		259	100	83	183	210	10	3	3	6	6

Traded to Detroit by Toronto with Frank Mahovlich, Pete Stemkowski and the rights to Carl Brewer for Norm Ullman, Paul Henderson and Floyd Smith, March 3, 1968. Traded with Wayne Connolly by Detroit to St. Louis for "Red" Berenson and Tim Ecclestone, February, 1971.

WORSLEY, LORNE JOHN (GUMP)

Born, Montreal, Que., May 14, 1929.
Goaltender. Shoots left. 5'7", 180 lbs.
Last amateur club: New York Rovers (Srs.).

			Regular Schedule				Playoffs			
Season	Club	Lea	GP	GA	SO	GAPG	GP	GA	SO	GAPG
1949-50	New Haven	AHL	2	4	0	2.00	—	—	—	—
1950-51a	St. Paul	USHL	64	184	*3	*2.88	4	9	0	*2.25
1951-52	Saskatoon	PCHL	66	206	*5	*3.07	13	31	*1	2.38
1952-53	Saskatoon	WHL	13	50	0	3.84	—	—	—	—
1952-53b	NY Rangers	NHL	50	153	2	3.06	—	—	—	—
1953-54cd	Vancouver	WHL	70	168	4	*2.40	12	29	0	*2.41
1954-55	NY Rangers	NHL	65	197	4	3.03	—	—	—	—
1955-56	NY Rangers	NHL	70	203	4	2.90	3	15	0	5.00
1956-57	NY Rangers	NHL	68	220	3	3.23	5	22	0	4.40
1957-58	Providence	AHL	25	83	0	3.32	—	—	—	—
1957-58	NY Rangers	NHL	37	84	4	2.32	6	28	0	4.67
1958-59	NY Rangers	NHL	66⅓	205	2	3.08	—	—	—	—
1959-60	Springfield	AHL	15	33	3	2.20	—	—	—	—
1959-60	NY Rangers	NHL	38⅓	137	0	3.57	—	—	—	—
1960-61	NY Rangers	NHL	58⅔	193	1	3.29	—	—	—	—
1961-62	NY Rangers	NHL	58⅔	174	2	2.97	6	22	0	3.67
1962-63	NY Rangers	NHL	65⅓	219	2	3.35	—	—	—	—
1963-64	Mtl. Canadiens	NHL	7⅓	22	1	3.00	—	—	—	—
1963-64	Quebec	AHL	47	128	5	2.72	9	29	0	3.22
1964-65	Quebec	AHL	37	101	2	2.69	—	—	—	—
1964-65	Mtl. Canadiens	NHL	18	50	1	2.78	8	14	*2	*1.75
1965-66ef	Mtl. Canadiens	NHL	48⅓	114	2	2.36	10	20	*1	*2.00
1966-67	Mtl. Canadiens	NHL	14⅔	47	1	3.18	1⅔	2	0	1.50
1967-68g	Mtl. Canadiens	NHL	37	73	6	1.98	11⅓	21	*1	1.88
1968-69	Mtl. Canadiens	NHL	28⅓	64	5	2.26	6⅙	14	0	2.27
1969-70	Mtl. Canadiens	NHL	6	14	0	2.33	—	—	—	—
1970-71	Minnesota	NHL	24	57	0	2.49				
	Minnesota	NHL	7½	20	1	2.65	3	14	0	4.67
		NHL Totals	768½	2246	41	2.91	60⅙	172	4	2.86

a Won USHL Outstanding Rookie Award and Charles Gardiner Memorial Trophy.
b Won Calder Memorial Trophy.
c Won WHL Most Valuable Player Award.
d Won WHL Leading Goalkeeper Award.
e Shared Vezina Trophy with Charlie Hodge.
f Received one assist.
g Shared Vezina Trophy with Rogatien Vachon.
Traded by **New York** with Dave Balon, Leon Rochefort and Len Ronson to **Montreal** for Jacques Plante, Phil Goyette and Don Marshall, June 4, 1963. Sold to **Minnesota** by **Montreal**, February 27, 1970.